We Were the Least of These

READING THE BIBLE *with* SURVIVORS OF SEXUAL ABUSE

Elaine A. Heath

Brazos Press
a division of Baker Publishing Group
Grand Rapids, Michigan

Published by Brazos Press
a division of Baker Publishing Group
P.O. Box 6287, Grand Rapids, MI 49516-6287
www.brazospress.com

Printed in the United States of America

Library of Congress Cataloging-in-Publication Data
Heath, Elaine A., 1954–
    We were the least of these : reading the Bible with survivors of sexual abuse
/ Elaine A. Heath.
        p.   cm.
    Includes bibliographical references (p.   ) and index.
    ISBN 978-1-58743-271-2 (pbk.)
    1. Sexual abuse victims—Prayers and devotions. 2. Bible—Meditations. I.
Title.
    BV4596.A2H43 2011
    242′.66—dc22   2010043982

11   12   13   14   15   16   17   7   6   5   4   3   2   1

For Morven

Contents

Acknowledgments

I would like to thank the many women and men who have trusted me with their stories and with whom I have journeyed in healing for the past twenty years. We have laughed, cried, and urged one another on through thick and thin. I especially want to thank my friend Dr. Morven Baker, director of the Ashland Women's Recovery Center. Morven was the first person I ever heard speak about sexual abuse in a church. She has been God's vessel of healing for countless survivors of sexual abuse and domestic violence.

I would also like to thank my sisters, Jeanine and Julie; my husband, Randy; and my colleagues Rebekah Miles, Jeanne Stevenson-Moessner, and Karen Baker-Fletcher for their continual support and wisdom as conversation partners during the writing of this book. I am indebted to my friends for their tireless intercessory prayer, especially Sherry.

Finally, I am grateful to my editors at Brazos Press who are kind, patient, insightful, and always encouraging.

Introduction

The process of healing from abuse is different for every survivor. While there are thresholds of healing that are common to survivors, every path to wholeness is unique. In this book we will consider several passages from the Bible that have proven to be profoundly healing for myself and other survivors with whom I have journeyed. Often in the chapters ahead I refer to "us survivors" and how "we" read a particular text. In doing so, I am referring to the actual survivors with whom I have experienced healing through that text. I do not presume to speak for every survivor everywhere or to think that my own experience or what I have written is the only way that people can heal.

To protect the privacy of persons involved, I have changed names and identifying details of the stories and individuals in this book, while preserving the issues, theological insights, and healing that took place.

While I am deeply grateful for the healing power of the Bible in my life and the lives of many others, for some survivors the Bible will never be accessible. In some cases it is virtually impossible for survivors to participate in religious practices, go to church, or read the Bible because of the residual effects of their trauma. The barriers to meaningful interaction with the text are even higher if they have experienced ritual abuse that uses religious objects in the abuse, or if the offender was a pastor, priest, youth leader, or Sunday school teacher. In these situations survivors' spiritual care involves the same respect, compassion, and encouragement any survivor needs. It is never appropriate to try to force someone to heal by using the Bible, prayer, church attendance, or other aspects of religion. We can be sure that in such cases the love of God is mediated with power as pastors, friends, and other caring persons incarnate the message of the gospel for the survivors, becoming the living text of love that survivors need. Love will heal many wounds that written words cannot. Indeed, without love the words of the Bible become "clanging gongs and crashing cymbals" (1 Cor. 13:1).

At the end of each chapter, I have included two sets of reflection questions, one set for survivors and another for companions of survivors, as well as a list of recommended activities. It is my hope and prayer that this book will help therapists, pastors, and survivors' loved ones to understand how the Bible can help to heal the wounds of sexual abuse. Most of all I pray that this book will bring hope, healing, and freedom to my sisters and brothers, the least of these.

1

We Were the Least of These

It was the middle of summer and I was preaching through a series entitled "Men, Women, and God." While the congregation was accepting of me as their pastor, they still tended to have patriarchal views about gender. Our church was in the Ohio River Valley, a region with unusually high rates of sexual abuse and domestic violence.[1] My goal in the sermon series was to introduce the congregation to deeper levels of the healing and liberating power of the gospel. As part of the larger goal, I wanted them to experience a reading of several biblical texts that could help to prevent and heal the sexual abuse and domestic violence in our city.

On this Sunday, several weeks into the series and after I had established a biblical foundation for gender equality, I preached about the sin of childhood sexual abuse. I talked about its presence even among Christians, its relationship to patriarchy, and how the church could help to prevent and heal this form of violence. My biblical text was the story of the woman at the well in John 4. The congregation was unusually quiet, listening intently as I preached about the woman's worth in God's eyes and how her series of rejections as an adult could very well have been the outcome of the wounds of sexual abuse. There were aspects of her adult life, I said, that are sometimes found in survivors of childhood sexual abuse. Instead of looking at her story as just one more example of an immoral woman, what if we thought about the kind of childhood experiences that can move a person toward this much chaos as an adult? This familiar story from the Gospels was a way to ease into a very difficult subject as we considered some of the consequences of childhood sexual abuse for adult survivors. As I spoke of survivors' struggle with perfectionism and anxiety, and other consequences of sexual abuse, I noticed several people had tears in their eyes.

Bringing the message to a close, I briefly mentioned the systemic layers of oppression that faced this woman and further isolated her from her own people and religious community. In short, I was linking the sin of childhood sexual abuse to the larger systemic issue of patriarchy. The good news, I said, is that this unnamed woman became the first evangelist. Jesus saw beyond the surface of her dysfunctional relationships to the misery of her life. More than that, he saw the person she could become. Jesus trusted her, wanted to drink from her cup, was willing to be seen talking to her. Jesus did not shame her. When Jesus met her, he saw someone who wanted to be a true worshiper. This woman was not doomed to live in the shadow of her abuse forever. Because of Jesus, she found her own voice and with it led others to the one who set her free.

After the benediction, I followed custom and greeted people as they were leaving the church. An older woman, Laura, lingered at the edge of the sanctuary. Her husband, Marty, had already gone out to the car. They were usually there on Sundays but kept to themselves and rarely came to fellowship events. I always thought their reticence was because they were new in town, having moved there just a year before I did. When we passed the peace, Laura stood still instead of moving into the aisle. She stared ahead and only greeted others if they first spoke to her. Marty was a little more outgoing, but not much. They were both tall and dignified. Nearly eighty, Laura was still strikingly beautiful, with her shoulder length white hair and stylish clothing.

When the last person had left the sanctuary, Laura approached. Taking my hand, she looked into my eyes and was silent, searching for the right words. Finally she spoke. "Pastor, what you preached about really touched me. For the first time in my life, and I have been going to church my entire life, I actually understood every word of the sermon."

"Thank you, Laura!" I said, surprised by her comments because she had been listening to my sermons for nearly two years. Why would she understand this sermon and not the others? There was something more that she seemed to want to say, so I waited.

With no change in facial expression or tone of voice, Laura matter-of-factly continued, "My neighbor and his friend raped me. Two of them, together, one after the other. They were in high school. I was seven years old." The words came out with no more emotion than if she were telling me what she had for dinner the night before. "I hadn't thought of it in a long time. Your sermon made me remember it." The faintest glimmer of pain began to show in her eyes. "I've never told anyone before," she whispered. That sermon marked the beginning of Laura's healing.

Today Laura experiences the love of God, laughs freely, and participates in Bible studies and outings with friends. She and Marty have become favorites of many of the younger adults at the church, who are often dinner guests at the couple's home. Although she is still reserved by nature, Laura has definitely found her voice, and she is a blessing to everyone around her. She is compassionate, a deep thinker, a joy to her friends.

Why Survivors Disconnect from the Church

As Laura explained in one of our many conversations after the disclosure of her abuse, prior to the advent of her healing, she had never been able to experience prayer or spiritual feelings the way other people seemed to. Although she is bright, she did not understand the Bible very well or desire to read it. When pastors stood up to preach, she disconnected. There was an internal block that she could not comprehend. Deep within her heart she longed to know God more fully, and she wanted to experience the love of God that others described. But doing so was not possible until she heard her own story of suffering within the biblical text and experienced a pastor who could validate her story and speak of it in terms of healing and redemption. She had to experience the gospel interpreted by a survivor.

Laura is only one of many survivors of abuse I have been privileged to know over the years in my roles of pastor, spiritual companion, retreat leader, professor, and friend. Her story is unique, yet in some ways Laura exemplifies people everywhere who have survived childhood sexual abuse. Often they are internally if not outwardly disconnected from Christianity, the church, the Bible, and clergy. Much of their alienation has to do with how the Bible is read and interpreted in the church. Some of it has to do with excessively gendered language for God in hymnody, prayers, and the liturgy. The church's obsession with sexual sin coupled with its poorly developed theology of sexuality only compound the alienation. (Many survivors, for example, think of the church's polarization around sexual orientation as being focused on the wrong set of questions. They believe that an orientation toward sexual violence, rather than toward a particular gender, is the orientation that is inherently sinful.)

Laura had been in the church for a lifetime, carrying the painful secret of her abuse, not knowing how it shaped the rest of her life, how it filled her with shame, how it erected barriers between herself and the love of God, how it prevented her from feeling safe and loved even with trustworthy people. No one ever spoke from the pulpit or anywhere else in the church about sexual abuse and its consequences. Laura experienced decades of patriarchal biblical interpretation that reinforced the message that men and their desires and needs are what matter the most. She had internalized the belief that the Bible teaches that women and girls exist to serve men, no matter how painful and dehumanizing that might be. All the God images that had been given to her were male. Inwardly, without knowing exactly why, she shut down whenever a man stepped into the pulpit and spoke of a male God, especially one who is all powerful. The Bible held no attraction to her, for it was the voice of a male God protecting male interests. Even though Laura was a moral person, she spent a lifetime feeling defective—feeling like an outsider in church and community because of her hidden shame.

Once Laura heard the good news of the gospel for survivors, once she realized how relevant the Bible was to her own story, her heart opened wide to the healing love of God. What then happened to her and what has happened to me and so many others I have known is nothing short of miraculous. Laura has come home to God and to herself. Laura's healing has taken time and has included many resources such as therapy, the cultivation of healthy friendships, and pastoral care. But the turning point for her was when the Bible was interpreted so that she could locate her specific suffering in its story of redemption. Laura was evangelized when the Bible was read through the eyes of a survivor.[2] Her evangelization was holistic, a process of initiation into a life of wholeness and wholehearted discipleship.

How many women and men are walking among us today bearing the wounds of sexual abuse, alienated from the God who longs to heal them, not knowing the power of the gospel because pastors and church members have not learned to read the Bible with survivors of sexual abuse? Imagine what it would mean if seminary curriculum required students to learn about sexual abuse and presented them with a hermeneutic of Scripture that was healing and liberating. Think of the impact the church could have in preventing and healing sexual violence. Think of the missional potential in introducing hurting people to the love of God. Could it be that one of the reasons the church is failing to evangelize people today is that we are not taking seriously the pervasive reality of sexual abuse and its consequences for survivors—that we are not offering them the good news they need to hear?

Waking Up

My vocation in ministry and as a theologian has emerged from my own journey into shalom. Like Laura, I am a survivor of sexual abuse. The awakening for my healing took place when one of my daughters was in the fifth grade. She brought a note home from school asking for parents' permission to allow students to see a film warning about the dangers of sexual predators. Parents were invited to come to school and preview the film before giving permission for their children to see it. I went to the school on the appointed night and watched the film along with other parents. The main vignette was about a little girl whose next-door neighbor, an older man, groomed her for sexual abuse. Because her parents were not paying attention and the child was vulnerable, she was victimized by the man next door. The film was vague enough to be appropriate for fifth graders but deeply disturbing to the other parents and myself.

As I walked home with a neighbor, she asked what I thought about the film and whether I would allow my daughter to see it. All of a sudden the words rushed out, surprising me with their stark truth. It was as if I were listening to someone else say, "I was that child. That is what happened to me." The woman looked at me, horrified, and didn't know what to say. I myself didn't know what to say. I could not believe I had told this neighbor, whom I scarcely knew, the darkest secret of my life. As soon as the words were uttered, a wave of shame engulfed me. I was glad for the darkness of the night so that she could not see my embarrassment. It would take years to come to terms with that shame and to be delivered from the feeling of uncleanness that had been put in me by my perpetrators.

Until then I had never given a name to what I had experienced as a child. One of the offenders was a pastor. His abuse damaged my view of Christianity and God in ways that would take decades to heal. The words *abuse, molested,* and *raped* were not words I used to describe my own experience to myself as the years went by. In fact, I did not articulate my own story of abuse to myself or other people. I remembered it at times but quickly moved those memories to the back of my mind and busied myself with the work at hand. Like many survivors, I was active in my church and a devoted mother to my children. I tried to be a "good person." I did not know how deeply anxiety and shame controlled my daily life because my eyes had not yet been opened to how the abuse had affected me. That night as I walked home from my children's school, I woke up. It was the beginning of my healing journey. It was the first time I honestly named what had happened to me when I was a child.

The major turning point in my spiritual healing came several years later. By this time I had been a Christian for twenty years and had experienced a measure of healing from the residual effects of the abuse. I had just begun seminary. One day I was doing some homework for one of my classes, having to do with Matthew 25. It was a familiar passage that I had practically memorized over the years, the parable of the sheep and goats. I came to the King's shocking words to a surprised humanity on the day of judgment: "Whatever you did to the least of these brothers of mine, you did to me" (Matt. 25:40 NIV).[3] And conversely, "Whatever you did not do for one of the least of these, you did not do for me" (Matt. 25:45 NIV).

I thought about the "least of these" and the male language saying that the least were "brothers." I wondered if sisters were included in that group. I thought they were, but the language specified brothers. Did "the least of these brothers of mine" mean that male disciples who were imprisoned, hungry, and naked were the least of these, or was the King talking *to* "the brothers" about their relationship to those who were imprisoned, hungry, and naked? The footnote in my Bible said the Greek was "the least of these brothers." The meaning seemed more open-ended in the footnote. What about babies and children, I wondered. Did they count as the least of these, or did a person have to be old enough to know Jesus to count as a disciple? Just who were the least of these?

I read the passage over and over, recalling images I saw daily on the news and in the city where I lived, people who were hungry, sick, strangers, lonely, and in need. I saw all kinds of people, male and female, young and old. I saw people of different ethnicities. As I envisioned the people, I heard the words "Whatever you do to the least of these, you do to me." Inside me the voice of Jesus said, "I am in the least of these. All of them."

Something shifted in me, as if I had been wearing someone else's glasses and I took them off and now could see clearly. This text was not about gender. It was not about religious insiders and outsiders. It was about the love of Jesus for all the "little ones." All of a sudden I saw Jesus *in* the suffering people, hidden with them in their obscurity, loving them and experiencing all their pain, even when they did not know he was there. The least of these were male and female, young and old. They were "neither Jew nor Greek, male nor female, slave nor free" (Gal. 3:26–28). Jesus was somehow in all of them, his presence determined not by faith choices on their part but by his infinite love for people.

Then without warning, right in the middle of seeing Jesus profoundly present in "the least of these," the memories of my abuse surfaced. The images flooded my mind, but this time, to my astonishment, I saw Jesus *with me and in me*, suffering everything. I saw his love for me, his unwillingness for me to suffer alone, and his judgment against the abuse. I felt his promise for a new life for me in the future, his determination to heal my wounds, his "no" to the shame and sin that scarred my life. It was my own experience of having Jesus say, "*Talitha cum*! Little girl, arise!" (Mark 5:41).

I felt like Lazarus rushing out into the light of day, his grave clothes trailing behind. I had been among the "least of these"! This text was not just for the "brothers" but for all the little ones, all who are vulnerable and at risk, who are confined and at the mercy of others. Jesus was with me, in me, for me, long before I could know it!

Recognizing my identity as the least of these changed my life. It set the trajectory for so much that would follow as I continued to live into God's call, move through my graduate education, ordination, and my ongoing endeavor to become the woman God created me to be. This experience opened me to a new way to read Scripture, one that was increasingly liberating and empowering as I learned to read Hebrew and Greek and completed doctoral studies in theology.

We Were the Least of These

We were the least of these, all of us who suffered abuse, neglect, violence of every kind. Jesus was with us; Jesus was in us; Jesus is for us. The stunning fact of Jesus's presence is the key to our healing and to understanding the biblical narrative of salvation. We were not alone. We are not alone. Jesus's experience of the cross has everything to do with our wounds and our sorrows. His resurrection from the dead is more than a creed we recite. It is a living power that lifts us out of the black holes of our lives, that heals our wounds, that removes our shame, that gives us "beauty for ashes, the oil of joy for mourning, a garment of praise instead of a spirit of heaviness" (Isa. 61:3). Because of Jesus the wounds of sexual abuse can heal.

In the chapters ahead, we will consider several key passages of the Bible that are good news for the least of these. Each of these narratives has been transformational in my life and in the lives of many survivors with whom I have journeyed. We will read the story of the fall, the Israelites' wandering in the wilderness, the narrative of the Levite's concubine, psalms of lament and healing, and stories of bleeding and broken women whom Jesus loved and healed. We will read the Bible with survivors of sexual abuse who know the meaning of Jesus's promise: "Behold, I make all things new" (Rev. 21:5).

For Reflection

For Survivors

1. Laura's healing began with a sermon in which she finally heard her own story. My healing began with previewing a film at my daughter's school. How did your healing journey begin?
2. When I read this chapter:
   a. I felt . . .
   b. I remembered . . .
   c. I hoped . . .
   d. I prayed . . .

For Those Who Journey with Us

1. When I think about using gender-inclusive language and images for God in the teaching, preaching, and worship resources in church:
   a. I feel . . .
   b. I think . . .
   c. I hope . . .
   d. I pray . . .

Recommended Activities

- Watch: *The Color Purple*
- Create: Paint, draw, or sculpt an image to express the promise of Revelation 21:5: "Behold, I am making all things new."

2

Fig Leaves

One of my early memories of Sunday school was when I was about seven years old. A nurse who worked the same shift with my mother at the veteran's hospital asked if she could take my brother and me with her to Sunday school. The teacher told the story of Adam and Eve, how God created them, how they disobeyed God, and how they lost their place in paradise. The story fascinated me with its talking snake, garden, and forbidden fruit. The teacher said the woman, Eve, talked to the snake. My mother was afraid of snakes. She would never have talked to it. She would have taken a hoe to it or shouted for my brother to come and kill it. When the teacher gave us a page to color, I was shocked to see a naked man and woman, their flesh barely concealed behind Eve's long hair and the well-placed shrubbery. None of my coloring books at home had naked people or talking snakes. I reached into the shoebox full of crayons, hoping the talking snake did not know where I lived.

Not a Children's Story

For many church people, the story of Adam and Eve has become little more than a fanciful children's story, the sort that you find in coloring books. The characters are simple line drawings. Preachers may add some color to the page, but the meaning is essentially black and white. God created a man, then a woman using the man's rib. God told them to live in the Garden of Eden and avoid one tree. They disobeyed God because they were proud, eating the forbidden fruit and releasing sin into the world. It was mostly the woman's fault since she listened to the snake.

I have heard pastors preach that the man was foolish for listening to his wife in the first place. He should have known better than to trust her. Women are more easily duped than men, the logic goes. They are more emotional, less rational, more easily seduced. And how could Adam, after all, resist his wife's feminine wiles? He was doomed. These are the sort of interpretations of the text that I had heard for the first twenty years that I was a Christian. It was basically the version of the story told to me by the Sunday school teacher when I was seven.

In graduate school, I learned many other approaches to the text. One of them was shaped by a feminist hermeneutic[1] of suspicion. In this approach, the fall narrative was explained as the first instance of the "Madonna and whore syndrome" in the Bible. Throughout the text, some feminists argued, women were defined according to their sexual roles as virgins, wives, mothers, and whores. Eve was the bad woman who tempted Adam to sin, and every woman after her was tainted just because she was female. On the other hand, Mary of Nazareth was good because she was a mother. Best of all, she was a perpetual virgin. Traditional understandings of these texts sexualized and dehumanized women, I was told. And I had to agree.

So much of what I had heard about gender in my early formation as a Christian had been demeaning toward women.

Some of it had been overt, but much had been subtle. It was unsettling to find myself agreeing with "the feminists and liberals" in graduate school, because for years I had heard pastors preach against "the feminists and their godless agenda" and against "the liberals and their secular humanism." I had been told that feminists and liberals rejected the authority of God's Word. They were post-Christian. They would ruin my faith. But what happened was the opposite. Feminist colleagues gave me permission to ask hard questions, and I came home to depths of faith and healing that otherwise would not have been possible.

Throughout my graduate education, I felt as if I were living on a boundary line between liberal and conservative, a foot in both worlds, fully at home in neither. Just as those pastors had warned me against feminists and liberals, in graduate school I encountered liberals and feminists who mocked all evangelicals as mindless fundamentalists who did not know how to read the Bible. It seemed they were tolerant of everyone and everything except evangelicals. Their sweeping generalities were just as harmful as the traditional interpretations some preachers promoted.

I did not want to caricature either side. Both sides had glaring weaknesses and important strengths. Why did there have to be only two sides? Why impose an artificial limit to perspectives when life is far more nuanced? Couldn't there be a civil conversation with many voices? God was leading me to another way of reading the Bible and doing theology, one that was beyond "liberal," "feminist," "conservative," and other labels.

The more I questioned the Bible's meaning and the more I expanded my investigation into alternate views of the text, the more powerful the Bible became in my life. Developing a hermeneutic of Scripture shaped by St. Irenaeus, Karl Barth, Julian of Norwich, and several other theologians, I increasingly experienced the Word of God as "living and active, sharper than a two-edged sword" (Heb. 4:12).

Foundational to my deeper reading of Scripture was the phrase Jesus had impressed upon me with so much healing power early in my theological education: "Whatever you did to the least of these you did to me." Knowing that Jesus is among the least of these revolutionized my reading of Scripture. I had always known the Hebrew prophets were oriented toward justice, but their emphasis on the least of these now became crystal clear. The concern for aliens, widows, and orphans had always been plain in the law of Moses, but now the reason for this care was more explicit. Christ was mystically present in the aliens, widows, and orphans. Whatever we did to them we did to Christ.

No text took on new meaning more than the story of Adam and Eve. When I read this familiar passage through a hermeneutic of "the least of these," it changed my theology of the atonement and how I understood salvation. It opened new vistas on the meaning of grace. But what really stunned me was the effect it had on my students when I began to teach about this text a few years later.

The class was a new one I had designed for doctor of ministry students intended to introduce them to the facts of domestic violence and sexual abuse and strategies for preventing and healing this kind of violence. None of the students had previous instruction in these topics, despite all of them having master of divinity degrees from good seminaries. The class was diverse in race, gender, and theological orientation. All of the students were in full-time ministry. Some of them had been pastors for many years.

As we read the story of Adam and Eve through the eyes of survivors, sensitive to the presence of Jesus in "the least of these," it was as if they were reading this story for the very first time. Instead of reading it as a story about guilty sinners, we read it as a narrative of abuse. In this story of violence against God's children, we found a paradigm for how original wounds of all kinds, not just of sexual abuse, eventually lead to the bondage of sin. Most importantly, we saw how God looks at sinners first and foremost as those who have been *sinned against*. Before Adam and Eve ever sinned, they were sinned against.[2] Their sin emerged from the wounds they received from the serpent and its deception.

The class was life changing for most of the students, in no small part because of this text. Some of them began their own healing journey from abuse they had never named before. Others began ministries to survivors of abuse and saw the focus of their pastoral ministries become more oriented toward healing in general. All of them came away from this text with changed understandings of sin. They began to look at sinners the way God does, as those who were sinned against before they passed that sin on to others. This perspective came by reading Adam and Eve's narrative through the eyes of a survivor.

Original Sin or Original Wound?

As we have already seen, the traditional reading of Genesis 3 focuses on the guilt and willfulness of Adam and Eve, on their sin in eating the fruit.[3] Their vulnerability and deceivability are minimized in that interpretation. Pride is the inclination attributed to them, leading to their fall. This is the premier text used to support the doctrine of original sin. Yet this familiar interpretation depends upon a Western reading of the text that is not universal to the church.

St. Irenaeus,[4] one of the greatest early theologians of the church, believed Adam and Eve were immature and that their fall was the result of immaturity more than premeditated sin. Julian of Norwich, a fourteenth-century Christian mystic and one of the greatest theologians of all time, also saw humanity[5] as exuberant and childlike, falling not out of malice or pride but out of a childish mistake. By the time I encountered St. Irenaeus and Julian of Norwich, I was firmly grounded in Jesus's love for the least of these. Their theology rang true to my experience both as a sinner and as a pastor holding forth the good news of salvation.

In the history of biblical interpretation, there have been many meanings ascribed to the narrative of the fall. Today more than a few theologians read the text as an etiology, a story that explains how humans move from childhood through sexual awakening into adulthood. That is, they move from being "naked and unashamed" to being mindful of their sexuality and possessing a desire to cover their nakedness. They move from undifferentiated human existence as children to gendered lives as men and women.[6] But when read through the eyes of survivors of sexual abuse, this story is about much more than sexual awakening. It is about sexuality awakened through deception, exploitation, and violence. It is a story of God's children robbed of innocence and set on a path of alienation. Violence of all kinds begins with this first experience of being sinned against. But thanks be to God, violence and abuse do not have the final word! For this in the end is a story of hope and redemption. It concludes with God's judgment against the serpent. The day will come, God says, when the head of the serpent will be crushed (Gen. 3:15). Its power will not last forever. Though Adam and Eve cannot go back to their Edenic life, God provides clothing and goes with them into the world they must now inhabit. Neither God's love nor God's presence are withdrawn. The end of Genesis 3 is the beginning of salvation history.

The New Reading

Let us turn to the story, then, and read it with survivors. In this new reading, we will follow St. Irenaeus and Julian of Norwich, envisioning Adam and Eve as immature persons who in their vulnerability and naïveté are the original "least of these."[7]

Before the fall, Adam and Eve are like children, naked and unashamed. They are playful and free in the abundant garden.

They live in peaceful community with one another and God. The only boundary given for them, according to the text, is the tree of knowledge of good and evil (Gen. 2:9). They are not to eat of its fruit, God warns, or they will die. Adam and Eve cannot know what "die" means, because they have not eaten of the tree. To know evil is to participate in it, which is something they have not done.[8]

Adam and Eve are blameless, naïve, beautiful, and like all children, capable of being deceived. They are vulnerable, which means they are capable of being wounded.

One day one of the other creatures speaks to them. Because they are innocent, they do not attribute evil motives to other creatures, nor do they fear them. God has not told them to avoid the serpent. They have only been warned to avoid the tree. Adam and Eve have "dominion" over the serpent, meaning they have agency and do not have to follow the serpent's instructions. To prey upon them it must deceive them.

The Bible lets us know that the serpent has evil motives but does not explain the origin of evil in the serpent.[9] Adam and Eve are trusting of the familiar creature that shares the garden. They are blind to the danger that lurks before them because of their naïveté, so they listen vulnerably to the serpent's deceiving speech.

Good parents do what they can to protect their children from predators. We show films to fifth graders to help them recognize the signs of a predatory adult. We teach young children about "good touch and bad touch." We no longer let our children go trick-or-treating on Halloween because they must not take candy from strangers. But the fact remains that despite all our warnings children have no way of knowing exactly what the danger is because they have not "eaten the fruit." They are the least of these, capable of being deceived. Little ones from every family are vulnerable to a serpent with a persuasive argument in its mouth and violence in its heart. The serpent comes in the guise of Daddy or Aunt Mary or the grandfatherly man next door.

The Bible says that Eve believed the serpent, saw the fruit was good, and wanted to be like the God who made her.[10] These are normal desires children have: to eat something sweet and to be like Mom or Dad. What is not normal, what is diabolical, is the manner in which the serpent manipulates Adam and Eve through their normal bodily appetites and familial affections. Deceived by the serpent's arguments, Eve takes the fruit and gives some to Adam, who is with her. Similarly, the vast majority of sexual abuse takes place through an enticement at the hands of a deceptive adult or older child known and trusted by the child.[11]

When Adam and Eve eat the fruit, they swallow a cancerous shame that begins with their sexuality. The leaf of the fig tree is irritating to human skin, not unlike stinging nettles. Adam and Eve press fig leaves against their genitals, covering their vulnerability with punishing leaves. The shame and pain of what has happened to them spread from their sexuality to every part of life. Their precious freedom to trust God, one another, and themselves is broken. Their unselfconscious playfulness is gone. The natural world that used to be a safe space is now filled with danger and threat. A sequence of death-dealing consequences is unleashed. No aspect of life is left untouched.

This is the death that God had warned about, a pervasive alienation from which all future violence would emerge. Oh the sorrow that would soon mark their lives! The consequences of their deception and abuse would now include a male drive to domineer over women and a female struggle with enmeshment and fear. Now Adam begins to define Eve, calling her Eve instead of *Isha*.[12] The original wound has become the source for patriarchy, the first systemic evil in the Bible. Because they were sinned against by the serpent, Adam and Eve have been caught in a terrible web of deception, wounds, and sin. These same dynamics will be handed on to subsequent generations. This is not a story about original sin as much as it is a story about original wounds.

The story of Adam and Eve is archetypal for every person who has suffered sexual abuse. Note, I am not saying that the "essence of sin" is sexual abuse. What I am saying is that child sexual abuse is paradigmatic for the process of all kinds of wounds leading to sin. Survivors have experienced the shattering of trust and pervasive shame. We know all too well the alienation that makes vulnerability and intimacy so hard. Fear, anxiety, and grief, the holistic trauma of abuse, all skew how survivors see ourselves, others, and the world. Our understandings of God are damaged, especially if the perpetrator is related to the church in some way. Out of this matrix of injury survivors of sexual abuse develop a broad array of coping strategies to find our way in life.[13] For some of us, perfectionism is a way to try to stop feeling defective. For others, the wounds are behind our attempt to control everyone and everything in life, in order to feel safe. Some of us suffer from addictions, promiscuity, and a multitude of destructive behaviors. Many of us go on to a lifetime of relationships that are abusive, dysfunctional, and chaotic, because of the residual effects of the original wounds.[14] We emerge from the abuse like Adam and Eve, toiling against thorns, laboring at life, yearning for love and security. Like Adam and Eve hiding behind painful fig leaves, we do not perceive that the face of God is the face of Love.

In our anxious and suffering state, God comes to us. Like a kind Mother, God exchanges soft clothing for the stinging fig leaves.[15] God our loving Shepherd leads us home. The good news of salvation is that Jesus was with us, among the least of these. He has made a way for us to experience shalom. The abuse does not have the last word. Jesus, not the abuse, not the serpent, not the shame, tells us the truth about who we are. We are children of God, created in God's image, chosen and beloved. Jesus wants us to know that his love will heal our wounds.

For Reflection

For Survivors

1. What are some of the interpretations you have heard of the story of Adam and Eve?
2. In what ways, if any, do you see the "Madonna and whore syndrome" in popular culture?
3. The idea that God looks at sin first from the standpoint of the sinned-against leads me to think . . .
4. When I imagine Adam and Eve as vulnerable children rather than rebellious adults . . .
5. My own version of wearing "fig leaves" has been to . . .

For Those Who Journey with Us

1. What are some of the interpretations you have heard of the story of Adam and Eve?
2. In what ways, if any, do you see the "Madonna and whore syndrome" in popular culture?
3. The idea that God looks at sin first from the standpoint of the sinned-against leads me to think . . .

4. When I imagine Adam and Eve as vulnerable children rather than rebellious adults . . .

Recommended Activities

- Watch: *Little Miss Sunshine*, *Forrest Gump*
- Create: Assemble a prayer table in your home that includes a candle, a photo of you as a child, and a card that says "I am chosen and beloved." For each chapter of this book that you read, add another item to your prayer center to represent the healing that you encounter in the chapter. If you do not have space to leave a prayer center set up, create a special prayer box or basket in which you place these objects. You can take them out to prepare an altar space for your prayer time, then put them away when you are finished.
- Discover: Visit a local art museum that has works depicting the stories of Genesis. How do the artists interpret these stories? How did their culture and social conditioning shape their interpretation?

3

Through the Wilderness

When those of us who were abused were children, our hearts and our boundaries were broken by the abuse. This means that our agency, our full power to say yes and no, was damaged. Ironically, this wound led to many of us becoming experts at reading and adapting to the people around us so that we could please them, while at the same time ignoring our own intuition as it shouted, "Get away from him! Watch out for her! Run!" Is it then any surprise that so many of us ended up in abusive relationships as adults? Those early broken boundaries put us on a path of greater vulnerability to charmers who turned out to be violent and oppressive. This tendency was true of the people we chose to marry, the kinds of faith communities we joined, and our work environments. The pattern repeated itself in all sorts of relationships. It is as if we were Adam and Eve eating new versions of bad fruit over and over because some new snake kept tricking us. And every time we realized we had done it yet again, the shame from the original wound deepened.

To make matters worse, as we struggled to understand and overcome these broken patterns, many of us were labeled and rejected by the church. This was because of our divorces, addictions, abortions, and other sorrows. We were told that sexual sins are different from other moral failures. Sexual addiction, promiscuity, adultery, fornication, anything having to do with broken sexual boundaries somehow left a permanent stain that even Jesus couldn't remove. We learned from a good many of our churches that divorced people were unfit to take communion, direct the choir, teach a Sunday school class, or be pastors. All of these rejections and pronouncements were made without a thought for what might have begotten such grief in our lives. The problem was diagnosed as sin, plain and simple, divorced from the actual stories of our lives. It wasn't just that we had sinned. We *were* sin. In all of this the Bible was used as punishment, as threat and blame and wrath. The toxic shame from the original abuse gained power with each successive judgment. Is it any wonder that so many survivors leave the church?

But God is very persistent, and despite all these obstacles, the Good Shepherd seeks and finds the lost sheep. Oh the astonishment we feel when we finally hear the real gospel, the Good News, when we hear God call our name! We are stunned to learn that God is our *Redeemer*, the One who *sets us free and heals our wounds*! When God leads us out of bondage it takes our breath away. There is so much to unlearn. There are glories ahead that we do not know. We cannot imagine our true dignity, or power, or grace. Like the Hebrew slaves fleeing through the Red Sea, we start our healing journey looking over our shoulders, vigilant, tired, and afraid. We do not know exactly where we are going. And at times, early on, despite our deliverance, we are inexplicably tempted back toward Egypt.

Into the Wilderness

That is exactly why we need the "pillar of cloud." That is why we must sojourn through the wilds. Our healing of boundaries is going to take some time and will not come without great struggle. We have to learn who God is and who we are. Recovery is a trip through the outback, an adventure that is perilous, beautiful, wild, unutterably holy.

In seminary, when you take introduction to the Old Testament, one of the first things you learn is that the exodus event is the central narrative of the Hebrew Bible. It is the pivotal event that reveals God's mercy and fierce compassion for humankind. Through the exodus, God's people are delivered from bondage in Egypt and are eventually given the Law, a new way of life that restores boundaries that slavery destroyed. The Law helps God's people learn to respect themselves again, and honor one another, and orient their lives in worship of the true God. The Law restores broken boundaries with creation, especially in Sabbath regulations. No aspect of life is left unhealed.

Liberation theology, we learn in systematic theology, is grounded in the exodus event. It is a theology in which salvation is the divinely orchestrated liberation of oppressed people and an oppressed earth. When I first heard of liberation theology, I thought it was "liberal" theology, with its focus on social justice and the earth. Was it some kind of Marxism dressed up in churchy clothes? Some of my friends thought so. But a deeper look convinced me that nothing is more evangelical than liberation. Isn't the Good News for all creation? Don't our own lives persuade us that sin is systemic as well as individual?

Some people call liberation theology a "theology from below" because it originates from experiences of marginalized people. I think of it as "theology from the least of these." There are many kinds of liberation theology, including black, Korean, Chinese, Latin American, feminist, and womanist perspectives. Liberation theology brings important gifts to those of us who are survivors, because it helps us to name our experience, frame our search for wholeness, and embrace more fully what redemption means. Slaves are "redeemed" when they are set free. They are bought out of slavery by the "redeemer." In liberation theology, there is much more emphasis on sin as systems of oppression that violate whole groups of people than on sin as individual spiritual alienation from God, so liberation theology also helps to correct hyper-individualism in theology. Black liberation theology is particularly linked to the exodus narrative because of the history of enslavement of African people.[1]

Many African American spirituals draw from the exodus event for images and archetypes of deliverance and empowerment. "Go Down Moses," for example, tells the story of Exodus 3 with a repeated emphasis on God commanding Moses not to fear but to confront Pharaoh and lead the people into freedom. "Tell old Pharaoh, let my people go!"[2] The final verse of the song bridges the gap from Exodus to Christ: "O let us all from bondage flee, and let us all in Christ be free."[3] That is what good liberation theology always does: it leads us to the Redeemer who sets the captives free.

A Road Map for Recovery

When read with survivors, the exodus narrative is a road map for recovery. Every major test in the wilderness is archetypal for the thresholds of healing God wants to bring us through as survivors. In so many ways we are like slaves learning to walk in freedom after a lifetime of bondage. Our journey is arduous and sometimes slow. The Redeemer won't let us off the hook. We have to learn that the real God is our God now, and our former gods are not. This means that we can no longer worship our old gods of relationships and achievements and possessions. Addictions to substances, to patterns of control and fear and perfectionism and passivity have to go. In the wilderness, we face our own hunger, thirst, and fatigue—elemental human need. Each time we do, we have a choice to return to the old ways of bondage or to walk in the newness that God offers. If we will cooperate, the wilderness sets us free. The wilderness gives back to us our own voice.

We have to learn who we really are: people of God, beloved, chosen, and called. We are not the property of other people, nor do we own those we love. In the wilderness, we come face-to-face with our enmeshments with other people, with our chameleon ways of merging into others to seek their approval. We see clearly the ways we thought we owned our children, our spouses, our friends. We come to see how the liberating mission of God in this world is manifested most powerfully through healthy, mutually enriching community. One relationship at a time, one experience at a time, we open our tightfisted grip, step back, and begin to love others in freedom. This is a wilderness journey because it is uncharted in our lives. It is a path into a frontier we never imagined possible.

Our self-sabotaging ways and our patterns of victimization and our fatalism about our condition are revealed in the brisk wilderness air for what they really are: the suffocating remnants of abuse. In the wilderness, we are tested repeatedly as we face memories, relationships, jobs, dreams, religion, and freedom. Again and again we are brought back to who God is and who we are. One step at a time we walk into shalom. We cannot do this without the pillar of cloud and fire.

The Cloud

The story of the pillar is found in Exodus 13:17–22. The Bible says that when Pharaoh finally releases the Hebrew people, God does not lead them in a direct route to the Promised Land, because that would take them through Philistine territory. God decides the best way to deliver them is to take them in a roundabout path through the wilderness so that they are not overwhelmed with the temptation to return to Egypt. The shortest route to the Promised Land, in other

29

words, is not the best route for them. By keeping the Hebrews out of Philistine territory, God spares them from having to flee from the Egyptian army and at the same time face warfare with Philistines, who surely would attack the vulnerable group. The frustratingly inefficient route the people must traverse is a carefully planned strategy on the part of the Redeemer. The goal is absolute liberation. The Redeemer has their backs. The Redeemer wants them to know they do not have to choose between the lesser of two evils—Egyptian oppression or Philistine violence. The Redeemer is charting a new way that is free from oppression.

To make the safer route utterly clear for the fleeing Hebrews, God provides a theophany, a physical manifestation of the divine presence. "The Lord went in front of them in a pillar of cloud by day, to lead them along the way, and in a pillar of fire by night, to give them light, so that they might travel by day and by night. Neither the pillar of cloud by day nor the pillar of fire by night left its place in front of the people" (Exod. 13:21–22).

In Exodus 13:17 there is a pun in the original language that is missed in most English translations, playing on the Hebrew word for "repent." God thinks the people might "change their minds and return" (repent) to Egypt if they have to face angry Philistines too early in their journey out of Egypt. Ordinarily we equate repentance with turning from wicked ways to the path of righteousness. In this case, God thinks the Hebrews will repent of their righteousness and return to Egyptian slavery if they are faced with too many tests of faith too soon![4] For survivors the wordplay is profound, because so many times we have to repent of loss of self, loss of courage, loss of agency. We have to repent of cooperating with our offenders in our own adult experiences of abuse. We have to choose to go into the foreign wilderness of healing. The temptation for us, especially early in our healing, is to repent of healing and go back to familiar bondage.

The language of repentance to describe the Hebrews' early struggle toward freedom is striking, for there is a deep spiritual core to the old life of bondage. We survivors have to embrace an ongoing conversion to our new life of freedom in Christ. That old bondage is related to whom and what we worshiped, that to which we gave ultimate authority in our lives. This is a spiritual problem. Even so, we cannot just leave Egypt, forget about it, and act as though that's the end of that. We have to learn to inhabit our holy freedom. When we set out with God, we have no idea of the extent to which we have lived our lives from broken boundaries. We cannot see just how much shame and fear have driven us. The wilderness is the place where God gradually shows us the truth. With each revelation God offers the way through to greater freedom. God's method is to lead us with a "cloud."

The story of Exodus is filled with supernatural phenomena: a burning bush, the ten plagues, a shepherd's staff that turns into a snake, water from a dry rock. In each of these phenomena, God uses ordinary, everyday elements but infuses them with divine power for the purpose of liberation. Some of these natural means of deliverance are elemental in a deeply symbolic way: earth clogging the wheels of the chariots, wind blowing to part the sea, water drowning the enemy, and fire blazing to illumine the night. God the Creator uses primordial elements of creation—earth, wind, water, and fire—to redeem and re-create his oppressed and broken people.[5] In our own journey from bondage to freedom God also uses natural elements infused with divine power. Nowhere is this more evident than in the "cloud" God gives to us.

The theophanic cloud is found in several other passages in the Bible, including 1 Kings 8:11, where God's glory fills the newly dedicated temple, and Isaiah's call vision (Isa. 6), where Isaiah is humbled and cleansed and sent forth in mission. In these and other passages, the theophanic cloud is God's way of calling people forward into a life of holiness. Sometimes the cloud references are fearsome, with God metaphorically riding on the clouds in a cosmic battle against evil (Ps. 18). Most of the Old Testament theophanic cloud references are linked to deliverance and holy empowerment.

In the New Testament, we find an extraordinary new image, one in which the cloud is human, "a great cloud of witnesses," all the faithful who have gone before us and are now cheering for us as we run the race of life (Heb. 12:1). Just as the natural elements of wind, water, and fire comprised the pillar of cloud in Exodus, the "cloud of witnesses" is a large body of real people whose job it is to cheer us on to faith and wholeness. Their light illumines our darkness. Their warmth brings comfort and hope on cold, hard days. Some of our "cloud" are indeed the saints, mystics, and martyrs who have literally gone before us in death. Their lives and writings are guides to us in the wilderness. But we need more than books and stories; we need a cloud that we can see and touch. God comes to us in the cloud of faithful, healing people today. It is the job of the church to be part of that cloud now, "while we are yet alive" as the old hymn says. It is the vocation of the church to manifest the divine presence leading people out of Egypt, through the wilderness, on to the Promised Land. This is our call as the church.

The Permanent Stain

A few months ago I was having dinner with some colleagues at a restaurant in Durham, North Carolina. Our server came back to our table frequently, asking if we would like more water even when our glasses were full. Finally he said, "I'm sorry I keep lingering around your table. I don't mean to eavesdrop, but I heard you talking about the Bible and faith, and I wondered if you are here for a conference or something."

"Yes, we are," we told him. "We are meeting at Duke University with the Wesleyan Theological Society, and we are from all over the United States." We each introduced ourselves and told where we were from.

His eyes lit up and he said, "I am a Christian too! I have been taking a theology class for a few weeks now and I really love it." We smiled and told him we were excited with him and asked him to tell us more about it. He described the class and the church he attended and how much he was learning. He said that he especially was interested in evangelism. Then I asked, "Are you planning to go into ministry? It sounds like you have a passion for sharing your faith."

"Oh, no," he said, his face falling and his voice trailing away. "I can't ever become a pastor." He shrugged his shoulders, embarrassed, his voice nearly a whisper. "I am divorced. You know what the Bible says about that." He turned away, starting to leave.

"Wait," I said, "there are other ways to understand those biblical texts. People get divorced for many reasons, sometimes because of violence, sometimes because a spouse cheated. It isn't so black and white. And doesn't Jesus forgive all our sin? You *can* be a pastor, and your experience of being divorced could be part of what makes you compassionate as a pastor. There are other churches that have different views about this. Look around. Don't give up." His expression of shock changed to hope and wonder as these words sank in. Then he had to leave. Other tables needed his help.

My colleagues and I looked at one another in amazement. Before the server confessed his reason for coming so often to our table, we had been talking about the problem of the church shaming and rejecting those who are divorced without contextualizing the problem in the fact of original wounds. We had been talking about the problem of "the permanent stain."

During Jesus's ministry, most people regarded those who are sexually broken as being permanently stained. But what did Jesus think? In the story of the woman taken in adultery, the one clear case where Jesus was asked to judge a sexual sin (oddly enough, the male half of the guilty party was not brought to Jesus for judgment), he asked the accusers who were without sin to cast the first stone. One by one they left. When Jesus was alone with the woman, he said to her, "Neither do I condemn you. Go and sin no more." Jesus did not see this woman's condition as a permanent stain (John 8:1–11). He did not think she was doomed to keep repeating the same mistakes over and over. We do not know what Jesus wrote when he knelt in the sand to respond to the woman's accusers. Could it be that he wrote "you are not your sin"?

Jesus the Key

For the Christian, Jesus is the hermeneutical key to the whole Bible. Unfortunately, in the history of biblical interpretation, the church has made some terrible mistakes. We have at times interpreted God as Sadistic Perpetrator of torture, genocide, racism, sexism, and the worst violence imaginable. We have, in fact, projected upon God our own darkness and have used that projection to justify heinous evil. This is why church history includes the Crusades, the Inquisition, Christians buying and selling slaves, colonialism, manifest destiny, and a long history of participation in violence against women and children.

Wherever we find an *interpretation* of Scripture that violates the liberating and healing spirit of Jesus in the Gospels, we have to go to Jesus to unlock the *real* meaning of that text. The apostle Paul wrote that Jesus is the "image of the invisible God," the One who shows us what God is doing, and the One who has the authority and power to reconcile all things that have been broken through sin (Col. 1:15–23).[6] A big part of our problem in theology is that we have rushed to assign labels to many things without going to Jesus the Redeemer to discern the actual problems. In our haste for certainty and control, we threw away humility and grace.

But mercy triumphs over judgment (James 2:13). Jesus is the Redeemer. He is the One who hears our cries, like those of the Hebrew slaves, who sees our bondage, who knows our weakness, who has loved us from the start. We were the least of these, and our Redeemer was with us. Our Redeemer knows the whole story.

Our Redeemer leads us through the wilderness where he delivers us from death one step at a time. It is our Redeemer's will to do this through his body, the church, the living cloud. When we who are the church live our true vocation, we *are* the Good News. We become Moses confronting Pharaoh, breaking down the hellish gates of abuse and all its consequences, shouting, "Let my people go!"

For Reflection

For Survivors

1. What would happen if we rejected "permanent stain" theology?
2. The woman who was taken in adultery was about to be stoned by her accusers. What are some of the ways we survivors stone ourselves?
3. Tell about a time you were tempted to "repent" of healing and "head back to Egypt."
4. As I reflect upon my own journey through the wilderness thus far:
   a. The greatest struggles have been . . .
   b. The "Moses" in my life has been . . .
   c. My own "cloud of witnesses" includes . . .

For Those Who Journey with Us

1. What would happen if we rejected "permanent stain" theology?
2. Some people think that if we believe and practice "mercy triumphing over judgment" we will trivialize

or minimize or even give up belief in the reality of sin and evil. Respond to this assumption.

3. The most challenging aspect of journeying through the wilderness with survivors is . . .

Recommended Activities

- Watch: *Diary of a Mad Black Woman*
- Create: Chart a map of your own journey through the wilderness on a large sheet of paper, noting the "pillar of cloud" and significant times of growth and of struggle.
- Read: *The Glass Castle* by Jeannette Walls

4

The Terrible Secret

Every semester when I teach Introduction to the Theory and Practice of Evangelism, I invite Jan Langbein to talk to my students. Jan is the executive director of Genesis Women's Shelter.[1] I want students to know that the church's engagement with social justice is one of its greatest responsibilities in evangelism, and no form of injustice is more widespread than domestic violence and sexual abuse. Jan and her team at Genesis offer hope and healing to thousands of people who suffer from abuse. While Jan is a Christian, Genesis reaches out to all persons regardless of their faith, race, ethnicity, gender, or sexual orientation, without pressure to change their religious beliefs in exchange for help. The people of Genesis Women's Shelter want everyone to know that God never condones abuse.

As Jan explains to my classes, many Christian women suffer from abuse in their marriages, including the most degrading forms of sexual abuse. Because their offenders are their Christian husbands, some of whom are even pastors, it is more difficult for these women to name to themselves or others the sexual violence they suffer. If the women were also sexually abused as children, their boundaries were already broken by that abuse, and they may think that sexual abuse is just part of "the way things are." In addition to these issues, the church has often taught that Christian women should submit to their husbands as the "head of the house." In many circles, women are taught that their husbands are the "spiritual head" and to disobey, resist, or refuse their husbands is to rebel against God. These women come to believe that they have to endure rape and other forms of sexual degradation if that is what their husbands want. To do otherwise, they learn, is to sin. Sexual violence goes on every day behind the closed doors of Christian homes, including among the most affluent and well-educated people in the world. It is a sin that knows no boundaries in terms of religion, race, class, socioeconomic status, or education.

"I have seen just about everything," Jan says. "I have seen women who were beaten, kicked, burned, bitten, raped with curling irons and every other kind of object you can imagine. Why do they stay in these relationships? One of the big reasons is they think God demands it."

Sexual abuse is evil no matter who the offender is. Pastors and Christian leaders must learn the facts about sexual abuse within marriage and must work to bring about the liberation and healing of survivors. Tragically, some of the women do not survive. They are like the Levite's concubine in the last three chapters of Judges.[2]

The Levite's Concubine

When we meet her in Judges 19, she has no name and does not speak. We only know her as "the Levite's concubine." She calls the Levite "husband," but to him she is subhuman, an object to use for sex and slave labor. She does not have the legal rights of a wife. She is the Levite's chattel property. She lives and dies in a nightmare of sexual violence, and none of it is redemptive. The story of her torture, rape, murder, mutilation, and the resulting civil war brings to a bloody climax the primary theme of Judges, summed up in its final verse: "In those days there was no king in Israel; all the people did what was right in their own eyes" (Judg. 21:25). Sexual violence is the ultimate manifestation of a conscience gone to hell.

In the last chapter, we thought about the healing journey of the Hebrew people as God led them from slavery in Egypt. We saw in their narrative the journey of healing we survivors must take in order to establish the boundaries that were broken by our abuse. The necessity of God's leadership through a divine "cloud" came home to us, and we reflected upon the "cloud of witnesses" that guides us home to God and ourselves. We considered the importance of a gradual wilderness journey in healing from the effects of our former bondage.

As we arrive in the book of Judges, we come to a new era for the Hebrew people, after they have settled in the Promised Land. Despite God's desire for their lives to be peaceful and abundant, once again the people live under oppression. Only this time, they have begotten the violence themselves. The cycles of stories in Judges are all the same. In each case, God's people have compromised themselves and God by turning away from the law of Moses. Their worldview, behavior, and spirituality are now shaped more by the violent world around them than by the Torah. Each story begins with intolerable suffering, not unlike the opening chapters of Exodus. The people cry out to God for forgiveness and healing, just as their ancestors did in Egypt. They repent for having forsaken God and the Law. God in mercy then raises up a "judge," a spiritual, civic, and military leader to help them throw off the oppression and reclaim their identity as God's people. After their deliverance, the people enjoy a relatively brief season of peace, then they abandon their faithfulness to God's ways and move back into an even worse subjugation to their enemies. Their repeating pattern results in a downward spiral of degeneration as the people of God lose their God-formed conscience. Increasingly, everyone does what is right in their own eyes. The horrific culmination of loss of conscience is the story of the Levite's concubine.

The first time I read this story I could not believe it was in the Bible. What did it mean? How could the Levite husband get away with these crimes? Was there a lesson we were supposed to take away from this story? If so, I could not figure it out. I was confused and repulsed and appalled, and I did not want my children to read it. Furthermore, the church's silence about it astonished me. I never heard sermons about this story or saw anything in Christian books or Sunday school materials. Later I discovered that theologians didn't say much about the concubine either. Interpreters traditionally read the concubine's story with only passing interest in her. Commentators typically treat the concubine as a backdrop for the "real" players in the story, the men.

The problem with this interpretation, as Phyllis Trible demonstrates, is that it misses the terrifying pathos of the story, the *woman's* story, which resonates with the lived experience of far too many of us today.[3] There is more to this story than the desires of the men or the violated hospitality codes (the usual interpretive focus). The muffled cries of the concubine must be heard. The church must "journey alongside the concubine,"[4] for she is one of the least of these and we have much to learn from her.

Everywoman

The concubine is Everywoman who lives with violence. She suffers physical, sexual, emotional, verbal, economic, and spiritual violence. She is archetypal for us women of faith, in particular, who attempt to leave abusive relationships only to find ourselves betrayed, hunted down, handed over, and silenced by husbands, churches, clergy, and families of origin. The very institutions that ought to protect our lives become coconspirators in our destruction.

Notice the relationships in the concubine's life. Her husband is a Levite, a man from, of all things, the priestly tribe. Levites are supposed to be the spiritual leaders of the community. She is betrayed into her abuser's hands by her father, to whom she has fled for refuge from her husband. Her purpose for fleeing is unclear. In two of the early texts of the Hebrew Bible (Masoretic[5] and Syriac[6]), it says that she "played the harlot," while two others (the Septuagint[7] and Old Latin[8]) say that she "became angry with him." Either of these readings is permissible.[9] This woman is utterly alone, without advocate or friend.

It is significant that she does not flee with a lover, which one might expect if she were adulterous. She returns to her childhood home, suggesting she is seeking comfort and protection. Her flight surely had strong cause, because she does not have the legal right to pursue a divorce, and the consequences for runaway slaves in her day could be catastrophic. She is like many Christian women who try to leave an abusive marriage, going to their family of origin for help. And as is the case today, the first place the abusive husband goes to find her is the concubine's parents' home. There he is treated with extra hospitality and given back the woman who has no voice.

As the Levite returns home after reclaiming his runaway concubine, they must spend the night in Gibeah. The old man there who offers sanctuary to the Levite and his concubine is a model of loyalty to the sacrosanct ancient Middle Eastern institution of hospitality. But his kindness is for men, not women. When village men come at night demanding to gang rape the Levite, a story disturbingly similar to that of Sodom and Gomorrah, the old man quickly offers them a substitute: his own virgin daughter and the concubine, to "ravish them and do whatever you want to them" (Judg. 19:24). The women have no voice and no agency. Only the needs and desires of the men are important. Due to a skewed perspective that is part of the loss of conscience, the women's lives are worth less than the institution of hospitality. "Hospitality" must be shown even to the wicked men by giving them what they want.

The Levite suddenly pushes the concubine out into the dark with the violent men, who torture and rape her until dawn. She falls unconscious at the old man's door, her hands thrust out to the threshold. Her husband, upon finding her in the morning, orders her to get up. There is no feeling for her, no thought for her. He then dismembers her body and sends the pieces around to various Hebrew tribes, but there are no negative consequences for him. According to the Septuagint, the concubine was found dead by her husband, but the Masoretic text does not say this. It uses nuanced language that suggests she may have been alive when her husband "took the knife" and dismembered her. It is the same unusual phrase that is used when Abraham "took the knife" to slay Isaac, only Isaac was spared by an angel.[10]

Her husband shifts the blame for her death to the men of Gibeah, civil war ensues, and six hundred more women are kidnapped and violated, their families murdered, and their lives given over to satisfy the desires of the men in power. The cycle of violence continues.

Loss of Conscience and the Least of These

Why did the author of the book of Judges end it this way? The concubine's suffering, the circumstances surrounding her death, and the subsequent carnage are the final proof of the author's point. Covenant-breakers are capable of any evil. For God's people who forsake the covenant and adapt to the violent culture around them, conscience progressively deforms into "everyone doing what is right in their own eyes." In Judges, conscience has shifted from the internalization of the Redeemer's healing love to the internalization of Canaanite depravity. The Levite, the concubine's father, the old man, and the men of Gibeah all "do what is right in their own eyes." They follow their evil conscience. The rape and plunder of the six hundred women and the destruction of their homes and families is the final "act of conscience." The only person in this story who is not allowed to do what is right in her own eyes is the concubine, who flees for safety. Her life and her body are objects to be used and thrown away. The author's terse, matter-of-fact reporting of these events only underscores the grim reality of it all.

The primary theme of the book of Judges is that we, the redeemed people of God, can progressively lose our conscience. When that happens, "the least of these" suffer. The violence committed against the concubine ought to be unthinkable among God's people. Institutions, even the institutions of family and marriage, should never be more precious than human life. But God's people have gone astray, worse than Sodom and Gomorrah, and there are no angels in this story to intervene. Every person in this story is part of Israel, part of the people of God, the redeemed. This story is a call for repentance and reformation. Will we, the readers, become the missing angels?

Our Story

For many of us survivors of adult sexual abuse, this is one of the most powerful stories in the Bible, because it is God's way of telling our story. It is God's way of telling the horror of victims of sexual violence who do not survive the abuse, and the horror of the church ignoring and in some ways helping to perpetuate the abuse. This narrative holds a mirror up to the church so that we can examine our conscience in regard to the least of these.

Many of us survivors see the concubine as a Christian woman who suffers violence at her husband's hands, all kinds

45

of violence including sexual abuse. We know too well that her Levite husband stands for our violent husbands who are sometimes pastors or lay leaders in the church. The concubine's father represents our family of origin that treats our offender well and tells us to take him back. They tell us he just needs more love, that his parents were mean to him, and that he never had a normal childhood. If we will be patient, he will come around, they say. Don't leave him. When we read about the old man of Gibeah, we see all the pastors and priests who have told us the abuse is our fault and told us to submit to our husbands even to the point of death.

And God have mercy, when we read about the men of Gibeah who act like Lot's neighbors, what we see are all of us whom God has led out of the Egypt of sin and bondage into a Promised Land, only to have given ourselves over to a new kind of depravity. They are all of us Christians who have bought into the oppressive systems of the powers and principalities. The men of Gibeah are our church that ought to model redemption from the curse of patriarchy but instead perpetuates the curse as the very will of God.

Neither patriarchy nor its inevitable sexual violence should have a place among the people of God. If we will give ourselves over to redemption from the curse of patriarchy, we will be able to write a new version of the story of the Levite's concubines who come to us. We will become the missing angels.

The New Story

In the new story, the survivor who leaves the abusive relationship will be offered refuge and healing love by her family of origin. They will listen to her pain, believe her, help her secure the resources she needs in order to rebuild her life. When the Levite shows up at the door, they will see and hear with eyes and ears of truth. They will not hand the survivor over for further abuse.

The clergy will mediate the presence of Christ to her and will be a companion to her in her healing journey, offering protection from the destructive theology of the men of Gibeah. The clergy will discern the evil of giving primacy to institutions when those institutions become agents of death that violate the sanctity of human life. In their teaching and preaching and pastoral care, the clergy will empower the survivor to "rightly interpret the word of truth" (2 Tim. 2:15) concerning her value and dignity as a person made in the image of God. They will help her receive the healing love of our Redeemer, and they will work alongside the Redeemer in his liberating grace.

What of the men of Gibeah in the new story we can live? What of the Levite himself? In the new story, the church will stand against oppression and violence. We will not excuse or cover up or endure sexual violence anymore. The Levite will not be allowed to hurt our sister anymore, or blame her for his evil, or treat her like a slave, or pass violence on to the next generation through her. In the new story, the Levite will finally have an opportunity to repent because we will hold him accountable for his crimes.

Why is this terrible story in the Bible? Because there is a terrible secret in the church. The Levite's concubine is God's way of telling us to write a new story with the way we live, a story in which we are the angels. Angels are messengers from God, bold and clear, bearing the Good News of the Redeemer. The new story is what this broken world has been waiting for. The real question is, what are *we* waiting for?

For Reflection

For Survivors

1. Who have been the "angels" in your life, the ones who *did* come with a message of hope and healing?
2. As I read this chapter:
   a. I felt . . .
   b. I remembered . . .
   c. I grieved . . .
   d. I prayed . . .

For Those Who Journey with Us

1. As I think about becoming one of the "missing angels" who bear the Good News of the Redeemer:
   a. I wonder . . .
   b. I hope . . .
   c. I remember . . .
   d. I pray . . .
2. Many people believe that any sexual activity, including sexual violence, is acceptable as long as it is between consenting adults. Respond to this belief.

Recommended Activities

- Watch: *The Joy Luck Club*, *Enough*, *Fried Green Tomatoes*
- Create: Make a drawing, painting, or sculpture of the new story of the Levite's concubine. Depict angels coming to her aid.
- Discover: Find out about the battered persons shelter in your community. Do they have brochures and other information, including speakers, who can resource your church? What kinds of donations do they need? Many people working in domestic violence shelters have never met Christians who understand and resist domestic violence using the Bible. They have only seen the Bible used to perpetuate oppression. Consider taking them a copy of this book.
- Read: *The Shack* by William Young

breasts, and hips. Ironically, this objectification of our bodies desecrates and defaces the beauty in all of us.

Queen Vashti and Queen Esther

The book of Esther can be read, among other ways, as a story about the sexist objectification of girls' and women's bodies (Vashti and Esther) and the racist objectification of a people (the Jews). These two forms of oppression—sexism and racism—are bound together. In both cases people are dehumanized, their bodies treated as commodities to judge, sell, buy, use, and throw away. Because humans are made in the image of God, the objectification and commodification of human life are blasphemous. Nowhere is this more blatant than in sex trafficking, sex tourism, and the production of child pornography, a trio of evils that often combine sexual and racial objectification.

The Bible tells us that in the days of the Persian Empire a king named Ahasuerus ruled over 127 provinces, from India to Ethiopia (Esther 1:1). Flaunting his wealth and power, the king threw a party that lasted for seven days, with opulent furnishings, endless flagons of wine, and more food than anyone could eat. All of his officials took part, as well as nobles, armies, and guests from far away. On the seventh day the inebriated king sent the eunuchs to fetch Queen Vashti, who, according to custom, lived in the women's quarters with the harem. Queen Vashti was renowned for her beauty. The king wanted to show off his lovely queen to all his drunken guests.

But Queen Vashti refused to come. The Bible does not say why she refused. Perhaps she did not want to be ogled by a crowd of drunken men. For survivors, Queen Vashti is a hero for refusing to allow her body to be displayed. King Ahasuerus, prompted by his advisor Memucan, interpreted Queen Vashti's boundaries as rebellion and decided to make her an example throughout the empire. If Queen Vashti wasn't punished, then every woman in the land would rebel against her husband, Memucan said (Esther 1:10–22). Chaos would ensue. There would "be no end of contempt and wrath" (Esther 1:18). The king agreed. Everyone needed to know that the men were the masters of their homes. Queen Vashti was summarily deposed from her position, humiliated, and sentenced to permanent seclusion. She would never see the king again or life outside the harem.

After Vashti's deposal, the king's advisors recommended a new queen be selected through a beauty pageant. "Let beautiful young virgins be sought out for the king," they said, and "let the king appoint commissioners in all the provinces of his kingdom to gather all the beautiful young virgins to the harem in the citadel of Susa under custody of Hegai, the king's eunuch, who is in charge of the women; let their cosmetic treatments be given them. And let the girl who pleases the king be queen instead of Vashti" (Esther 2:2–4).

When children learn about this story in Sunday school, they usually receive a culturally conditioned interpretation in which young women willingly compete for first place in the king's beauty contest, not unlike a Miss America pageant. The winner gets to be queen! Children learn about Esther being the "fairest in the land," just like Snow White. After a lengthy preparation in which Esther is treated to special food, lotions, and clothes, the king picks her, and she joyfully becomes the queen. Eventually she uses her position to save her Uncle Mordecai and God's people. Everyone lives happily ever after.

But the story is much darker than that. It is not a children's fairy tale. For survivors whose abuse includes some form of child pornography or sex trafficking, this is a narrative of their suffering. No pubescent girl is safe from the king's commissioners, who forcibly take any beautiful virgin they find. Vulnerable girls, including Esther, are at risk because they are young, female, virginal, and beautiful. Like thousands of adolescent girls in Bangkok who are sold through sex tourism, Esther and the other virgins are unable to protect themselves from their captors. Their bodies and faces are commodities for the king to use. Every one of the "contestants" in this pageant will lose her virginity to the king and have to live for the rest of her life in the king's harem. Her body will be there for the king to use when he wants to. Like child prostitutes in Cambodia, whose johns are mostly white American or European men, Esther's ethnicity makes her even more vulnerable to exploitation and abuse.

An Epidemic of Human Trafficking

Sex trafficking and sex tourism are multibillion-dollar international industries. Sex trafficking is the buying and selling of people for purposes of sexual exploitation. Sex tourism is a practice in which adults travel to foreign countries in order to buy sexual encounters. While people of all races and both genders are victimized, approximately 80 percent of victims are female and 50 percent are children.[1] Children as young as toddlers are bought and sold for sexual exploitation by others. As many as two million women and children are in captivity as sexual slaves at any given time, according to UNICEF (the United Nations Children's Fund).[2]

Some of the victims are kidnapped, some are deceived into responding to advertising for nanny or domestic jobs overseas, and some are sold into bondage by family or friends. The suffering of those who are enslaved is beyond words. According to the United States Health and Human Services fact sheet on sex trafficking:

> Victims endure torture, rape, isolation, and starvation. They endure as many as forty-five sexual encounters a day. Health risks to the victims include drug and alcohol addiction; physical injuries such as broken bones, concussions, burns, vaginal and anal tearing; traumatic brain injury resulting in memory

loss, dizziness, headaches, numbness; sexually transmitted diseases such as HIV/AIDS, gonorrhea, syphilis, UTIs, pubic lice; sterility, miscarriages, menstrual problems; other diseases such as TB, hepatitis, malaria, pneumonia; and forced or coerced abortions. Psychological harms include mind/body/separation/disassociated ego states, shame, grief, fear, distrust, hatred of men, self-hatred, suicide, and suicidal thoughts. Victims are at risk for Post-traumatic Stress Disorder including acute anxiety, depression, insomnia, physical hyper-alertness, and self-loathing that is long-lasting and resistant to change. Victims often die young from tuberculosis, drug addiction, or sexually transmitted diseases such as AIDS.[3]

Sex trafficking, sex tourism, and child pornography are inevitable outcomes of the objectifying sins of sexism and racism. The story of Esther and Vashti can help us to think about the pain of those who are being reduced to a commodity, from our daughters who are being socialized to look like Barbie dolls, to the unspeakable crimes of child pornography, sex trafficking, and sex tourism. This story also helps us survivors see in the struggles of Esther and Vashti our own history of being objectified and God's empowerment of us to reclaim full personhood.

Nadia's Story

Nadia was twelve years old when her family moved to a small Midwestern town. They were among the "working poor," with two parents whose combined income still wasn't enough to pay the bills. Added to the economic stress of Nadia's family was the pain of alcoholism. As is typical of many children of alcoholics, Nadia grew up having to function as an adult, taking care of siblings, housework, and cooking, which left her emotionally vulnerable to predatory adults. She was a quiet and well-behaved girl at school.

Not long after moving into the tiny brick bungalow, Nadia and her mother met the neighbor across the street. It was a beautiful June day, and he was out tending his roses. They had come home from the grocery store and were taking the bags into the house when the neighbor walked over to say hello. He was a soft-spoken, grandfatherly man. After making small talk and extending a warm welcome to the newcomers, he surprised Nadia with an invitation. "Could my wife and I take Nadia to Sunday school and church with us?" he asked her mother. "We don't have any children of our own, and we would enjoy having her with us on Sundays." Nadia's mother agreed that it would be fine for Nadia to go to church.

The next Sunday Nadia was ready an hour before the neighbors, Mr. and Mrs. Granger, came to get her. It made her feel important that they wanted her company. The church was small and shabby, with friendly people who greeted Nadia with great warmth. Within a few weeks she felt as if she had always been a part of the church, with its tiny youth group and wheezing organ. The sense of community was for her sheer joy.

Meanwhile, Mr. and Mrs. Granger became friendlier than ever. Mrs. Granger invited Nadia to lunch sometimes and began to teach her to embroider. Nadia was aware that Mrs. Granger was lonely. It made her feel wonderful to be the object of special delight for Mrs. Granger. She enjoyed the fresh peanut butter cookies and the embroidery lessons. But what really excited her was Mr. Granger's photography studio.

Mr. Granger was retired, but he supplemented his pension with income from his hobby. The studio was in a separate building, a converted garage. Many of the townspeople came to him for wedding or graduation photos. Mr. Granger began to invite Nadia to spend entire afternoons with him in the studio, learning to develop film, use different lenses on the camera, and adjust the lighting for photo shoots. She loved learning all these new skills and enjoyed the supply of bubble gum Mr. Granger always had for her. As he explained various techniques for the equipment and talked to her about all the people he had photographed, he often stood close to her, his hand on her shoulder or waist. He often complimented her on her looks.

One day when Mrs. Granger was away shopping, Mr. Granger asked Nadia if she ever thought about being a model. She blushed and stammered that she wasn't pretty enough for that. He protested, saying she was the loveliest seventh grader he had ever seen. He continued in his gentle, persuasive voice until Nadia agreed to let him photograph her.

Mr. Granger shot many photos of her that afternoon, similar to the graduation photos he did for high school seniors. "Next time we'll try you in some different outfits, just like a model," he said. By the time Mrs. Granger returned from her shopping trip, Nadia was heading home for dinner.

Over the next few weeks, Mr. Granger often asked to photograph Nadia. He had assorted garments for her to wear for the pictures. When Nadia asked why he had the clothing, he said it was left over from a catalog shoot. Nadia felt more important than ever, as if she might really become a model in the future. One day Mrs. Granger was gone to visit a friend in the hospital. When Nadia came into the studio, Mr. Granger asked her to step into the house for a moment. She went in, wondering if Mrs. Granger had left a plate of her favorite cookies. Once inside he walked toward the bathroom. "I have a bubble bath ready for you," he said. "I would love to take your picture surrounded by bubbles. Would you let me do that? We'll arrange the bubbles so that nothing shows but your beautiful face." The camera equipment was already set up. Terrified and confused, Nadia ran home.

For the next several Sundays she found excuses not to go to church with the Grangers. Then school started and she threw herself into her new classes, trying to forget about Mr. Granger and his church. One day when Nadia was in math class, the principal's secretary came to the door, asking to see Nadia. "Bring your belongings with you, please," she said in a worried voice. Nadia followed the secretary to the office, where her mother and two men in dark suits were waiting for her. Nadia's mother's eyes were swollen from crying.

Half an hour later Nadia was at the police station in a room with a darkened window. The man politely asked Nadia if she had ever posed for Mr. Granger. Before she could answer, he emptied a large envelope onto the table. In front of her were several photographs of a girl about her size and age, naked, her body twisted into grotesque positions. The girl's face was not clear. With dawning horror Nadia realized that the detective thought she was the girl in the pictures. The detective's voice grew aggressive. "Well, did you? You might as well admit it," he said, towering over her, pointing to the pictures. "You know you did it!"

Nauseous at the images before her, Nadia stammered in protest. "I let him take pictures of me but not like that!" she cried. Where was her mother? And why was the window made of dark glass? No matter how much she told the man that she was not in the photos, he disbelieved her.

Threatening to lock her up unless she told the truth, the man insisted that she sign a confession. "Mr. Granger took these photos of you!" he shouted. "Admit it!" He slammed his fist on the table the way Nadia's father did when he was drunk.

Nadia broke down and wept, refusing to sign, unable to escape her tormenter. Filled with shame for having trusted Mr. Granger in the first place, she huddled in her chair, shaking. Finally the door opened and the other man said, "That'll be enough, Ted." Nadia heard her mother's voice in the background saying, "She's telling the truth. I would know if she was lying." Her mother had been on the other side of the dark window, watching and listening to every word. Nadia's mother took her to the car, mute. They rode home in shocked silence and never spoke of it again. Nadia learned later that Mr. Granger was arrested and convicted for making and selling pornographic images of children. His specialty was girls the age, size, and complexion of Nadia. Though grateful that she escaped what could have been an even worse victimization, it took decades for Nadia to heal from the shame and fear put into her by Mr. Granger, the detective, the images of porn she was forced to view during her interrogation, and her mother's inability to respond in a protective and healing way. Like the girls and women in the story of Esther, Nadia was sexualized and groomed by a predator.

The story of Esther and Vashti has helped Nadia to heal from habitually taking a "victim" stance, or passively accepting injustice in her adult life. She began by identifying with Esther's and Vashti's oppression and subsequently identified more with their resistance to it. In time, Nadia realized that her story could become a source of healing and hope for others. She came to see that, like Esther, God had called her to be an advocate for others. Today she is a lawyer who advocates for victims of violence.

The Objectification of the Jews

Just like Esther, who was taken captive by the king's commissioners and brought into the harem, her people, the Jews, lived at risk under an oppressive regime. As is the case in many parts of the world today, a dictator (in this case King Ahasuerus) wielded his power to launch an "ethnic cleansing." Because of the danger to Esther should her ethnicity be discovered, like many Jewish people during the Holocaust, her uncle Mordecai advised her not to reveal that she was Jewish (Esther 2:10, 19–20). Esther's exceptional beauty caused her to find favor with the eunuch in charge of the pageant, and Esther soon had a coterie of maids, advancing to first place in the harem. Yet she lived with the constant anxiety of being found out as a Jewish girl.

In time, a wicked and arrogant court official named Haman ascended to a position of power over Mordecai, who also worked for the court. When Haman demanded that subordinates bow down before him, Mordecai practiced civil disobedience. Just as Vashti had refused to disgrace herself with the king's drunken guests, Mordecai would not compromise his faith or dignity and bow down to Haman. Furious, Haman then devised a plot to destroy not only Mordecai but all the Jews. As he learned about the impending pogrom, Mordecai sent a secret message to Esther asking for her intervention.

An elaborate plan took shape, with Esther eventually risking her life to bring the plot to the king's attention. In the end, Haman was hanged on the gallows he had prepared for Mordecai, and the pogrom was averted. Mordecai was rewarded for his good citizenship, and the Jews were empowered to fight against their enemies. The Feast of Purim is a commemoration of this story, celebrating "the days on which the Jews gained relief from their enemies, and as the month that had been turned for them from sorrow into gladness and from mourning into a holiday" (Esther 9:22).

What makes this story so inspiring for survivors like Nadia is Esther's part in the empowerment of Mordecai and the Jews to resist their oppressors. Esther uses the power she gains as queen to resist injustice. When Mordecai sends a message to Esther about Haman's plot, he says, "Who knows? Perhaps you have come to royal dignity for just such a time as this" (Esther 4:14).

Like Nadia, many of us survivors are "wounded healers." We find joy in using our voices, skills, and life experiences in order to bring justice and liberation to others who have been oppressed through sexism and racism—through violence involving the objectification of our bodies. Like Mordecai and Esther, we believe that "for such a time as this" God is placing us strategically so that we can help other survivors heal and so that we can work to prevent such violence from happening to others.

For Such a Time as This

My colleague Dr. Nate Hearne grew up in rural Texas during the civil rights movement. Though he became a star athlete in high school, he was barred from the white section of restaurants and made to sit in the balcony of the theater away from white moviegoers. He endured much abuse at school during forced desegregation. The Ku Klux Klan was active in rural Texas. Some of Nate's relatives died at the hands of lynch mobs. Much of the time black men and boys who were lynched were sexualized, as in the 1955 torture and murder of a boy named Emmett Till,[4] the precious teenager whose death was the heinous event that launched the civil rights movement.

During this time, a widely read study was published on Americans' obsessive fears about "miscegenation," or the mixing of races. Sociologist Gunnar Myrdal discovered that southern whites believed that the main thing blacks wanted from integration was to be able to have sex with whites and to marry whites. Intermarriage was actually the last thing that black Americans wanted, according to the study, but that fact did nothing to dispel sexualized racism against black Americans.[5] Myrdal's study provided statistical evidence of an evil that black Americans knew too well: the widespread sexual objectification of blacks by whites. The blasphemous institution of slavery in America was the beginning of sexual objectification of black women and men in this country.

Today Nate draws compassion and wisdom from the terrible experiences he endured to identify with people who are objectified and exploited for any reason—economic disadvantage, race, sexuality, or immigration status. As an ordained minister and a public school administrator who works with at-risk students, Nate has become a powerful agent of healing "for such a time as this."

As Nate and I and some of our friends work together in ministry, we observe many parallels between the wounds of

61

racism and the wounds of sexual abuse. Both of these sins impart deep shame into those who are victimized. Both involve the objectification, sexualization, and dehumanization of people. In the story of Esther, we see the pain of all people who suffer from these wounds. We also see hope for healing. Through Vashti's integrity, Esther's courage, and Mordecai's political stance, we are challenged to work on behalf of those who are at risk. Christ has called us for such a time as this.

For Reflection

For Survivors

1. What are some of the ways you were socialized into your gender as a child?
2. As you look around now at television, movies, magazines, and the internet, how do you see the objectification of women's bodies being played out? How are men's bodies objectified? What about the bodies of people of color?
3. Have you ever felt like Vashti? Esther? Mordecai? The virgins who were taken to the harem but did not become the queen?
4. As I read Nadia's story:
   a. I felt . . .
   b. I remembered . . .
   c. I grieved . . .
   d. I prayed . . .

For Those Who Journey with Us

1. What are some of the ways you were socialized into your gender as a child?

2. As you look around now at television, movies, magazines, and the internet, how do you see the objectification of women's bodies being played out? How are men's bodies objectified? What about the bodies of people of color?
3. What can we do in the church to raise awareness of the evils of sex trafficking, sex tourism, and child pornography? How can your church become involved in helping others to heal from these forms of abuse?
4. As I read Nadia's story:
   a. I felt . . .
   b. I remembered . . .
   c. I grieved . . .
   d. I prayed . . .

Recommended Activities

- Watch: *Slum Dog Millionaire, Roots, The Color Purple*
- Discover: Do some research on the internet and find out how your denomination might be involved in helping persons who have been victimized by sex trafficking. Decide on one step that you can take to make a difference, such as a financial contribution, writing a short article for your church newsletter, or giving a talk on this topic in an adult Sunday school class.
- Observe: Visit an art museum in a metropolitan area to look at images of the biblical story of Esther, or view images online. How did the artists interpret the story of Esther according to cultural conditioning? Were any of the paintings sensitive to the story from Esther's or Vashti's perspective? How would you portray their stories artistically?
- Read: *Good News about Injustice* by Gary A. Haugen

6

Prayers of Lament and Mercy

There were seven of us gathered at my friend's house where we were learning to share our lives and pray together. Our group had met only a few times, so we were still getting to know one another and developing trust. We had been thinking about the Linns' wonderful book on the prayer of discernment, *Sleeping with Bread*.[1] As we moved around the circle, we talked about what we had been holding on to that was not life giving. Edith, well into her eighties, said, "I need prayer to help me let go of wanting to punish my enemies. This has been a lifelong struggle for me. But I think God wants me to be merciful in my attitude. God sends rain on the just and the unjust. I don't think God wants me sitting around wishing I could hurt people."

The other women nodded, listening. Edith was from Virginia, a coal miner's daughter whose slow drawl and homey wisdom were always a comfort. We were impressed with Edith's desire to become more merciful and less vindictive toward those who hurt her. A few minutes later the conversation turned to a recent event involving conflict in our community. Edith said, "I have been praying for God to give laryngitis to those hateful people who have been saying such terrible racist things and stirring up all this trouble!"

Marlene interrupted, "Edith! How can you say that? You just asked us to pray for you to be merciful, and now you tell us you are praying for people to get laryngitis!"

"Oh, I'm getting better," Edith said. "I used to pray they would get hemorrhoids." The room exploded in laughter, but Edith continued in earnest. "No, really, you can pray that way. I read it in the Bible!" Edith was right. This kind of prayer is in the Bible. In fact, the prayer book of the Bible—the Psalms—is riddled with what scholars call imprecatory prayer. Edith would call it hollering.

A Different Kind of Prayer

Edith practiced the kind of prayer we survivors need the most and yet find virtually absent from the church. She hollered to God about her frustration, hurt, anger, and sorrow over the racist words that cut into her life and our community. Because Edith prayed honestly about how she felt, asking God to give hemorrhoids to her enemies, she was gradually moving toward a desire to pray mercy for them. That is, the process of forgiveness was working itself out in her organically, naturally, as she prayed the honest feelings of outrage that she had toward offenders. In my own life and for so many people whose lives are healing from abuse, learning to holler in prayer is essential. We cannot heal spiritually without it.

The best way to learn this kind of prayer is to read a psalm every day as part of your spiritual practice. Don't just pick and choose your favorites, and don't overdo it. Stick with just one a day, like vitamins, and be systematic. Start with Psalm 1 (the "make me like a tree, God" psalm) and read through to Psalm 150 (the "let's throw a huge party for God" psalm). When you get to the end, go back to the beginning. You can get through the Psalter two times in a year this way, even if you miss some days. If possible, read the psalm aloud with a lot of expression. You may want to try singing a psalm occasionally, making up the melody as you go, because the Psalms were meant to be sung. Some of us even dance a psalm at times when we are alone with God in prayer. The more drama, the better!

We survivors have discovered that praying this way with the Psalms reconnects us with the full range of our emotions and helps us tell our whole life story to God, from the depths of utter despair (Ps. 88) to the heights of exuberant joy (Ps. 148). As we regularly, systematically pray the Psalms, we not only begin to pray them as our own experiences and feelings, but we also find ourselves praying them for the world. The Psalms are the great connector to the human condition. Eventually, they help us relinquish to God vindication for the wrongs that we have suffered. The long, slow process of forgiveness cannot begin without honestly taking stock of the offense. The Psalms help us to do this.

Because they underscore life's anxiety, chaos, and trouble, many of the Psalms could have been written by us survivors while we move through the wilderness of healing. For example, Psalm 57 begins, "Be merciful to me, O God, be merciful to me, for in you my soul takes refuge; in the shadow of your wings I will take refuge, until the destroying storms pass by. I cry to God Most High, to God who fulfills his purpose for me. He will send from heaven and save me, he will put to shame those who trample on me." This is the visceral prayer of a survivor whose adult relationships are destructive, as she takes steps to choose a life-giving path. The psalm continues with language about the enemy being like a greedy lion devouring human prey. These are the actual feelings of the "Levite's concubines" today.

Notice in this psalm that there is no effort to sanitize the language or pray for mercy for enemies. Instead, the psalmist visualizes in prayer the complete self-destruction of the enemy. "They set a net for my steps; my soul was bowed down. They dug a pit in my path, but they have fallen into it themselves" (v. 6). Survivors who face legal battles to keep their children when they divorce because of abuse, or who face a judgmental church in the same situation, find courage, strength, and faith in praying these words from the Bible. We know what it is like to have a pit dug in our paths. So we move through our recovery praying and weeping and hollering to God, "Let our enemies fall into their own traps!" We pray our way toward justice and peace.

Psalm 18:31–42 is even bolder, with the psalmist moving from defense to offense in pursuing the enemies and taking them down:

> For who is God except the LORD? And who is a rock besides our God?—the God who girded me with strength, and made my way safe. He made my feet like the feet of a deer, and set me secure on the heights. He trains my hands for war, so that my arms can bend a bow of bronze. You have given me the shield of your salvation, and your right hand has supported me; your help has made me great. You gave me a wide place for my steps under me, and my feet did not slip. I pursued my enemies and overtook them; and did not turn back until they were consumed. I struck them down, so that they were not able to rise; they fell under my feet. For you girded me with strength for the battle; You made my enemies turn their backs to me, and those who hated me I destroyed. They cried for help, but there was no one to save them; they cried to the LORD, but he did not answer them. I beat them fine, like dust before the wind; I cast them out like the mire of the streets.

Many feminist theologians and clergy are uncomfortable with this kind of militaristic language in prayer or liturgy, feeling that such language promotes religious violence and triumphalism. I have heard some of them say that this kind of language is especially inappropriate for survivors of abuse because we survivors have seen enough violence. It is true that militaristic language in the Bible has been misused far too often as part of the abuse of power in churches and governments. I am one of the feminists who critique the *misuse* of these biblical themes. But for me and many other survivors, this warrior language can be deeply healing. Psalm 18 helps us to fight for our lives, regaining that which was stolen and lost in the abuse. This is a song of resistance against injustice. It gives us language that helps us transition from being a victim and an object to becoming the strong, courageous, powerful people God calls us to be.

Numb and Silent No More

It is essential that we survivors reclaim our feelings and our voices. Many of us learned to "numb out" the terror, anger, confusion, and pain that we felt as children, and we continued those patterns of not feeling as adults. One congregant, Brianna, told me she has "credit card emotions." That is, emotions are absent when it would be "normal" to feel them, only to have them pop up in future installments at inappropriate times. She can be with her abusive father at a family gathering without feeling anything, but in the Hallmark store when she passes Father's Day cards she is filled with rage. The Psalms are helping Brianna heal from "credit card emotions."

In addition to learning not to feel, most of us were silenced in one way or another. In some cases when we tried to tell adults what was happening to us, we were not believed, so we stopped telling our truth. Others of us were blamed for our abuse as if we had "seduced" our offenders, and we were punished for telling the truth, so we stopped saying our truth. Many of us told about the abuse indirectly through nightmares, vaginal infections, phobias, eating disorders, and cutting ourselves, but the adults who were supposed to protect us missed the signals. They did not hear these cries of abuse. This is why a major part of our healing is

69

about gaining the courage and confidence to speak with our own voices, tell our truth, and be heard. Feeling our true feelings and speaking our reality are foundational for living in freedom. Through Psalm 18 and others like it, we reconnect with our feelings and voices about the worst things we experienced long ago and the struggle we face now as we live into wholeness. Telling the truth is the ground of all real prayer.

Thoughts of Mercy

This is why the entire Psalter is important. If we were to pray only the "imprecatory" portions of Psalms, we would be like a car with one wheel missing. We would drive off the road and into a ditch. Quite honestly, many of us do get stuck in painful memories, bitterness, and fear. But we are not our painful memories, nor do we have to be driven by anger and fear. As we systematically pray through the book of Psalms, we also pray psalms of repentance for ways in which we have hurt ourselves and other people. Gradually, ever so slowly, when we come to the imprecatory texts, we begin to think of the "enemies" as more than those who need to be held responsible for their sin. We begin to recognize that our greatest obstacles to peace are internal.

That is when Psalm 18 takes on a new dimension of meaning. The enemies that we pursue and beat into fine dust so they cannot rise again are shame, anxiety, and despair. The enemy is our self-sabotaging habit. It is our pattern of choosing a victim stance. As we pray with Psalm 18 about these most pernicious enemies, we find divine energy to help us move forward to a new way of life.

Eventually, honestly, almost unconsciously as we continue to heal and we continue to pray through the Psalter, we find ourselves, like Edith, having surprising thoughts of mercy toward people who have offended us. As Edith did, we begin to ask God to help us let go of the desire to hurt those who hurt us. In the context of a small, trusting group of spiritual friends, this process can take place more quickly. The healing process has its own time line for each survivor. None of us can tell others how fast to move forward, especially with the slow process of forgiveness. But all of us can help one another tell the truth in prayer and in life.

One of the ways we survivors can deepen in our prayer with the Psalms is to begin writing our own psalms of lament and healing. We can adapt a psalm from the Bible, personalizing it for ourselves, or we can write a new psalm. The following psalm is one that I wrote many years ago. In this psalm I express the healing power I have found in the prayer of tears. As you will see, lament and hope, sorrow and joy are bound together. The act of writing the psalm brought additional peace and freedom to me, as did reading it many times afterward.

Altar Tears

Altar tears.
Hot and holy, consecrated, eucharistic,
Rain of heaven, wordless words.
Intercessions, celebrations, weeping groaning,
Wild with keening, deep petitions, whispered
    thanking.
Grief and joy comingled,
Freely flowing,
Running down.

Altar tears.
Fountain streaming molten love through
Eyes of one upon whose life
God's consolation
Drips like honey,
Myrrh and honey, sweet, comingled, freely flowing,
Running down.

Altar tears.
Tears of trembling, holy trembling
In the regions of the self
Where God sows in barefoot feet,
Gently plants the Spirit seed
In faithing furrows of the soul.
Plants the seed of altar tears,
Grief and joy,
Myrrh and honey,
Sweet, comingled, freely flowing,
Running down.[2]

Psalms is not only our prayer book and hymnal in the Bible, it is also a part of God's Word that helps us to become honest with ourselves. In the manner of Edith, as we learn to pray through the Psalter regularly, faithfully, we find ourselves coming home to deeper truth about ourselves and others. And as Jesus promised in John 8:32, the truth sets us free.

For Reflection

For Survivors

1. What does it mean to find our own voices?
2. As I read through Psalm 18 slowly:
   a. The phrase or image that speaks to me the most is . . .
   b. It speaks to me because . . .
   c. I am challenged by . . .

For Those Who Journey with Us

1. What would happen if we included imprecatory prayer in public worship liturgies?
2. What is your understanding of the process of forgiveness?
3. As I read through Psalm 18 slowly:
   a. The phrase or image that speaks to me the most is . . .
   b. It speaks to me because . . .
   c. I am challenged by . . .

Recommended Activities

- Watch: *The Secret Life of Bees*
- Create: Write a prayer, psalm, or song that expresses your own deep struggle toward freedom and healing.
- Read: *Traveling Mercies* by Anne Lamott

7

Are You My Mother?

When my daughter was in prekindergarten, one of her favorite books was *Are You My Mother?*[1] Bedtime that year included countless readings of this tale of a young bird that hatches while its mother is out looking for food. The baby bird leaves the nest and goes in search of his mother on foot, but he passes her because he doesn't recognize her, never having seen her. He goes on to meet a kitten, a hen, a dog, and a cow, asking each of them if they are his mother. Their responses range from sympathy to shaming the little guy for his ignorance and need. Anxiety builds with each rejection, as the young bird frantically continues his search. He moves from living creatures to machines, seeking maternal love in a car, a boat, and a plane. Finally he comes to a "snort," a track hoe with a shovel. Suddenly, in a moment that induces sheer terror, the snort scoops up the hatchling that is too young to fly, but instead of hurting him it deposits him back in his nest. Just then his mother arrives, bringing love and his first meal.

One of the reasons this story is so engaging for young children is that it is normal for children to feel anxiety at separation from their mothers. As children read this story, they identify with the little bird's need to be with his mother. They identify with the fear the bird has when he is alone. It is not surprising that my daughter wanted to read this book with me again and again during the year she started school. Prekindergarten was a large, uncharted universe in which she had to leave home and be away from me for a few hours each day. This story took on liturgical importance for her, as a means of assurance that she would go out into the larger world, meet other people, see strange new school equipment and activities, but that at the end of the day she would come home and I would be there with love and something good to eat. The ritual of reading this book assured my daughter that when we were apart, I was still "there." She was not motherless.

Feeling Like a Motherless Child

"Sometimes I feel like a motherless child," goes the old spiritual, expressing one of the deepest wounds many survivors bear. There are several reasons for our haunting loneliness for Mother. In some cases, we suffered incest by our mothers, the ultimate maternal violation and abandonment. Others of us were abused by fathers, brothers, or grandfathers, and our mothers either did not know or would not act to protect us. Some of us told our mothers we were being abused, but our mothers told us we were imagining things, or they blamed and punished us. In some cases, our mothers just weren't around. They were at work or asleep or high. Whether our mother wounds were inflicted through willful abuse or unintentionally because economic hardship meant working two jobs and leaving the children to fend for themselves, our mothers were not there to protect us. The pain of their absence runs deep.

One survivor, Tunisha, told me that she grew up yearning for her mother's presence. While her mother worked long hours, Tunisha took care of younger siblings and herself. Tunisha confessed that often while her mother was gone she would put her mother's housecoat on, crawl into her mother's bed, and wrap her arms around her mother's pillow, breathing deeply of her mother's fragrance. She would pretend that her mother was there, holding her. Most of the time there was no other way to physically touch her mother, who neither knew about Tunisha's abuse nor seemed to realize how lonely and anxious her children were.

The feeling of being a motherless child is complex. We survivors describe it with some of these words: lonely, unwanted, afraid, hungry for affirmation, cold, anxious, confused, grieving, empty, uncertain, tentative, abandoned, overwhelmed, having to be tough, vigilant, unable to trust, trusting too soon, rootless, and homeless. Many of us are like that little bird, running and looking and calling for a good, wise, loving, present mother, but we don't know what she looks like or how to find her. Some of us latch on to our spouses, lovers, friends, or children, and none of them can be anyone other than who they are. One way or another they each have to say, "Your love is suffocating me." Our clutching, demands, disappointments, and attendant anxieties about our dysfunctions are exhausting. At times our steely grip on others brings about the thing we fear the most—the death of the relationship.

Some of us move from clinging to living creatures to the same things the little bird tried—cars, boats, planes, material wealth—but the emptiness remains. We are searching for God our Mother.

Searching for God Our Mother

Around the same time my daughter was in prekindergarten, I began attending a women's spiritual formation group at a

Pentecostal church. The teacher, Betty, believed that every word in the Bible trembled with incipient life for those who had ears to hear, so she told us that we should read and pray with the whole Bible, not just our favorite parts. She taught us to read, meditate, pray with, and live into the text, an ancient prayer practice that I learned much later has a Latin name: *lectio divina*.[2] So it was that I began trudging through 1 Chronicles, with its long lists of begats. Much of what I read seemed tedious and repetitive, especially the genealogies, but the beauty and wisdom of Betty's life convinced me that I should read and pray with the Bible the way she explained. With each passage I would read slowly, wait for a word or idea to surface, pray and meditate with what surfaced, and then ask God to help me live according to what came to me through the text. Sometimes I wrote the word or phrase on an index card and put it on the refrigerator with a magnet or in my purse so I could read it later.

It was nearly impossible to pray with the genealogies in the Bible, whose purpose I did not understand until I studied the Old Testament in seminary. Here and there, however, a tiny story was embedded in the list of begats. So it was that one day I came to 1 Chronicles 4:9–10 and a story jumped from the page. There was a man whose mother *named* him after her pain! This was a story I could pray with. As I read it slowly, my heart was filled with grief, for in Jabez I recognized all of us survivors who are looking for God's mother love.[3]

Taking Away the Curse

With a bitter wordplay Jabez's mother names him after her suffering. (The Hebrew word for pain is "jazeb.")[4] We know nothing else about Jabez's mother except that she suffers. Ancient Hebrew readers would understand that a negative spiritual force is released upon Jabez in his mother's naming of him. Spoken words were not just words but active powers that could bring forth consequences.[5] That is, Jabez's name is actually a curse placed on him by his mother.[6]

While the Bible does not say exactly how Jabez experienced the curse, the implication is that his pain caused him to cry out to God for deliverance. So we can conclude that he was in some kind of bondage. Jabez would not pray for God to bless and protect him from pain and suffering (the curse of his name and his identity) if he did not suffer anxiety. Neither would he pray for his borders to "be enlarged" if he was not in some way confined. Were his bondage and anxiety geographic, emotional, spiritual, or relational? There are hints in the two-verse story.

Notice the nuanced phrase: "he was more honored than his brothers." Was Jabez, like Joseph, the target of his jealous brothers' abuse? Some of us survivors respond to the embedded shame of our abuse by becoming high achievers, by being "good girls." We are perfectionistic and we make sure we know and follow all the rules so we don't get in trouble. Was Jabez like that? In shame-based families, it is common for children to have roles, including the star and the black sheep. Maybe Jabez was the star. He was honored more than his brothers, and that can be big trouble for a survivor who is a younger sibling.

Was Jabez a younger brother like David, honored yet rejected, anointed but hunted down? The text does not tell us. What it does suggest is that he was favorably singled out from his brothers by the community. Sibling rivalry and resentment from the less-favored brethren is a common theme in Old Testament narratives: Cain and Abel, Isaac and Ishmael, Jacob and Esau, the list goes on. Survivors read this story and wonder, could it be that his brothers were part of Jabez's pain? Did Jabez suffer abuse at their hands?

Even though he is born under a curse, Jabez has faith in the Redeemer. He turns to God, who has the power to uncurse. Jabez cries out to be delivered from pain. Furthermore, he asks for a blessing, the kind of blessing his mother did not give him, the kind that a good mother gives. Jabez's prayer is the most important thing he does. It is the essence of who he is. It is the secret to his liberation from the curse. God's word to Jabez is yes.

Several years after my first discovery of Jabez, I was at a conference with Fr. Adrian van Kaam, an extraordinary Dutch priest and scholar who developed a groundbreaking integrative approach to spirituality and psychological development called Formative Spirituality.[7] Fr. Van Kaam's original research emerged from his experiences of smuggling food to Jews in hiding during World War II. He was interested in the effects of trauma on faith formation. A group of us were discussing the effects of childhood abuse on our ability to become intimate with God as adults. I had noticed that some of the survivors with whom I have journeyed seemed to be closer to God in prayer than many Christians who had never suffered abuse. I asked Fr. Van Kaam, "Do you think that somehow survivors of childhood abuse find it easier to be intimate with God than persons who have never experienced abuse?"

Fr. Van Kaam paused for a moment then said, "Sometimes it is harder for those who have always known the healthy love of mother and father to differentiate between God and their parents, and this limits their perception of God. God is not much bigger than mother and father." He went on to explain that as survivors heal from abuse, as we realize who God is, we are much less likely to confuse God with our parents, and for many survivors the capacity for intimacy with God is very deep indeed. Fr. Van Kaam said that the ability to perceive and relate to diverse images of God is increased because we do not limit our understanding of God only to "Father." All of this, of course, is dependent upon ongoing spiritual healing and growth into freedom. The story of Jabez helps those of us who inherit our mothers' pain with that process.

Eating the Bread of Jabez

We survivors need to companion Jabez, which literally means to "eat bread with" him, for many of us were born into our mothers' pain. We are searching for the Mother love of God. At church we hear that God is omnipotent, omniscient, omnipresent, and omni-*male*. We see male clergy, deacons, elders, and board members. We sing songs with male language to describe a male Trinity, and we refer to ourselves, men and women alike, as the "sons of God." When we approach the communion table, we are served by men who tell us about the masculine love of God. When we gather the courage to raise questions about being born again from a male God, we are warned against the pagan feminists and told not to question the Word of God. Yet the Word of God contradicts the homogenous male God image. The Bible corrects this skewed notion of God as male, healing us with images of God our Mother.

The ball and chain of mother wounds, that peculiar shame of being that was handed on to us, will not be broken by the Male Warrior or the Male Judge or the Male Parent or any other exclusively male image for God. The key to our unshackling is the blessed face of Mother, the ferocious protection, the sweet kiss of mother love.

On my desk is a beautiful figurine from Central America, a brown-skinned mother standing in the center of her children, who encircle her legs with their embrace. A baby is securely held on her back in a colorful embroidered cloth, her little face peeping over her mother's shoulder. The mother holds a large basket full of bread. There is plenty to go around. Her face is turned outward, gazing toward the horizon. She is peaceful, strong, kind, fearless. The figurine was a gift from my husband, who said, "I think this will remind you of God." It has become an icon for me and for others who come to my office for spiritual companioning (bread sharing). It is a reminder to us of the Mother love of God.

There are many images of God in the Bible, none of them sufficient to exhaustively disclose the nature of God. One of the images is Mother. "Can a woman forget her nursing child, or show no compassion for the child of her womb?" God asks wounded people in Isaiah 49:15. "Even these may forget," God answers, "yet I will not forget you. . . . I have inscribed you on the palms of my hands. Your walls are continually before me" (Isa. 49:15b–16).[8]

We survivors are like Jabez, looking at the scarred, outstretched hands of Mother God, who reaches inside the broken walls of our lives, deeper than the pain, the memories, the grief, the everything. "As a mother comforts her child, so I will comfort you," whispers God our Mother (Isa. 66:13), God with bread and eyes that see all, God with a baby on her back.

We see God's mother love in Jesus, writes the fourteenth-century theologian Julian of Norwich. "For this is that property in God which opposes good to evil, so Jesus Christ, who opposes good to evil, is our true Mother. We have our being from him, where the foundation of motherhood begins, with all the sweet protection of love which endlessly follows."[9]

Some Christians become angry if you suggest that God is our Mother as well as our Father. "That is heresy!" they shout. "God is Father and only Father!" They address God as Father God and seem unable to comprehend that God might also be our Mother. They seem not to understand that God is much bigger than all the images God has given us in the Bible.[10] Nor do they perceive that when God is presented as an all-male trio, it leaves the impression that God literally is male, a position Jesus refutes in John 4:24: "God is Spirit." The Trinity is perichoretic, not sexual, and not gendered.[11] The belief that God the Trinity is male, rather than transcending gender, can contribute to a culture of violence against women and children, for it is a patriarchal belief that privileges maleness over femaleness, as discussed earlier in this book.

The question of God as our Mother as well as our Father arises from the depths of human suffering, from loneliness, anxiety, hunger, and despair, of survivors. It is a question whose biblical answer could help many others to heal as well. "Are you my Mother, God?" many of us have asked. "Do you love me as a kind Mother? If I am born again, does that mean that you are the one who spiritually birthed me? And if that is true, does this mean I can receive the motherly love from you that has been missing in my life because of my abuse?"

The Word become flesh is the Word of uncursing to all whose identities have been forged in our mothers' pain. Jesus brings Mother love to us directly, in prayer. He comes to us in the strength and kindness of the women in our lives—our sisters, daughters, and friends. The healing that Jesus brings is even big enough to bridge the gulf we felt between our mothers and ourselves. Safely held in the love of Jesus, we come to understand that our mothers were once "the least of these," with their own burdens and sorrows. Their absence, their neglect, their sin had its origin in their own story of suffering. Mercy triumphs over judgment, and though no one can replace our mothers and no one can remove the fact of our Jabez beginnings, we find that God's Mother love is enough. We heal.

For Reflection

For Survivors

1. Who are the people in your life who demonstrate the motherly love of God to you?
2. What are some ways you, like the little bird in the story, have been disappointed as you looked for motherly love from people and things that could not provide it?
3. When I read that God is like a nursing mother, and that God has my name imprinted in God's hands:
   a. I feel . . .
   b. I imagine . . .
   c. I wonder . . .
   d. I pray . . .

For Those Who Journey with Us

1. Why are so many Christian leaders afraid to think about or speak of God as Mother in addition to God as Father?
2. Who are the people in your life who demonstrate the motherly love of God to you?

3. What are some ways you, like the little bird in the story, have been disappointed as you looked for motherly love from people and things that could not provide it?
4. When I read that God is like a nursing mother, and that God has my name imprinted in God's hands:
   a. I feel . . .
   b. I imagine . . .
   c. I wonder . . .
   d. I pray . . .

Recommended Activities

- Watch: *How to Make an American Quilt*
- Create: Draw, paint, or sculpt an image representing God's hands with your name imprinted in God's palms.
- Read: *The Red Tent* by Anita Diamant

8

Eunuchs

Some people call the book of Isaiah the Gospel of the Old Testament because so much of this major prophet's work points to the coming Messiah. Often these promises are framed as great contrasts and healing reversals for those who suffer. For example, the people who walk in darkness will see a great light, declares Isaiah 9:2. A green shoot will sprout from a dry stump, he proclaims, a branch that will be resplendent with wisdom and knowledge and fear of the Lord (Isa. 11:1). The coming Messiah will reverse notions of kingly majesty, Isaiah prophesies, for he will be a Suffering Servant, wounded for our transgressions and bruised for our iniquities. He will heal us and bring us peace through his crushing experiences of grief (Isa. 53).

Many famous works of art have been inspired by these "contrast and reversal" texts of Isaiah. Nineteenth-century Quaker artist Edward Hicks painted more than a hundred renditions of the peaceable kingdom, pastoral images in which lions and lambs recline together and a child plays unharmed near a serpent (Isa. 11:6–9). G. F. Handel's *Messiah* draws heavily from the book of Isaiah. Like the peaceable kingdom text, many of the passages Handel set to music involve transformations for oppressed and oppressor. Every valley (the lowly) will be exalted and, every mountain (the proud) will be brought low. When the Messiah comes, Isaiah declares, his name shall be called Wonderful Counselor, the Mighty God, the Everlasting Father, the Prince of Peace (Isa. 9:6). For wisdom, justice, and peace will finally prevail (Isa. 40:4).

All of these promises are powerful for "the least of these." We see Edward Hicks's painting of the child playing safely by the serpent and our hearts ache for that day to come, for we have known the serpent's fangs and we want children everywhere to be safe. As we survivors move from being bound by shame and oppression into freedom as God's beloved children, we gradually experience valleys being exalted in our own lives. We love the choral power of the *Messiah* as we hear vast choirs sing the vision of the Lamb, who is worthy of our worship, for we have known his redeeming love. But among all the promises of Isaiah that speak to us survivors, one of the most precious is the prophecy for eunuchs:

> Do not let the foreigner joined to the LORD say, "The LORD will surely separate me from his people"; and do not let the eunuch say, "I am just a dry tree." For thus says the LORD: To the eunuchs who keep my Sabbaths, who choose the things that please me and hold fast my covenant, I will give, in my house and within my walls, a monument and a name better than sons and daughters; I will give them an everlasting name that shall not be cut off. (Isa. 56:3–5)

The Suffering of Eunuchs

Why would a promise to eunuchs matter so much to survivors? There are two kinds of eunuchs in the Old Testament. One meaning of the word simply refers to men who were trusted attendants to the king, some of them married. An example of this kind of eunuch is Potiphar in Genesis 39:1. But the predominant meaning of eunuch in the Bible is a man who has been emasculated through damaged, dismembered, or mutilated genitals. While sometimes eunuchs were born with genital disabilities, much of the time the condition was imposed upon them through slavery, war, or other intentional acts of subjugation. Eunuchs were used to guard king's harems and to serve as guards and advisors to queens. Because they were unable to sire offspring, they could be trusted to be in close proximity to the crown. This was the case with the eunuch who was the chief financial officer for Queen Candace in Acts 8. Most eunuchs, however, did not enjoy the privileges of royal appointments.

In the New Testament, Jesus referred to persons who intentionally remained single and celibate as eunuchs "for the kingdom of heaven," (Matt. 19:12). In this case, they chose to resist cultural norms of marriage and family in order to serve God's missional purposes in the world. While this third, positive kind of eunuch is important for our discussion at hand, the prophesies of Isaiah for eunuchs were directed toward those who bore a permanent sexual wound, one that was bound to a socially constructed identity of shame and exclusion.

As is the case for sexually ambiguous people today in mainstream culture,[1] eunuchs' lives in the ancient Middle East were often marked with loathing and exclusion. Ancient societies valued male virility, especially in the production of offspring. Effeminate men or emasculated men were the butt of jokes and other forms of abuse, then as now. The eunuch embodied "shame, impotence, and social deviance. His ambiguous, abnormal sexuality marked him as a threatening liminal figure."[2] The ancient Greek historian Herodotus (fifth century BCE) describes a eunuch with contempt, as "a thing of nought," while second-century Assyrian writer Lucian judges them "monstrous, alien to human nature."[3]

In Jewish culture, the sexual wounds of eunuchs carried profound spiritual implications. By law eunuchs were excluded from the worship assembly and were forbidden from serving in the priesthood (Deut. 23:1; Lev. 21:17–21). Like hemorrhaging women, it did not matter how or why they received their disfigurement. They were rendered permanently, spiritually unclean by their sexual wound. Even the most basic element of male Jewish identity—circumcision—was not possible for many Gentile eunuchs who might wish to become Jewish, because of the extent of their mutilation.

Thus, in many ways, eunuchs were men whose entire lives had been determined by a sexual wound. They were literally cut off from their own sexuality, sometimes at a very young age, so that the rest of their lives could be exploited. Eunuchs were men whose bodies were sexually colonized by others. Nothing they could do could restore them to shalom.

The Eunuch as a Type of Survivor

This is exactly how many of us survivors feel about ourselves, especially those of us who bear profound physical consequences from our abuse and those who find it nearly impossible to heal from our psychological and emotional wounds. For some of us, our sexuality was cut off when we were young and defenseless. We were robbed of a normal process of sexual development. Our minds were filled with images and painful memories linking sex to abuse. Our bodies were taken for others to use, and we have borne many consequences that have left us with the pain and suffering of the eunuch. Not only have our bodies and minds borne permanent damage, but for many of us exclusion, judgment, and labeling remain as consequences of the trajectories of our lives that emerged from our original wounds. Though Christ has forgiven our sin and is healing us of our trauma, much of the church looks at our sexual histories and declares our permanent unfitness for full inclusion in God's house. We experience the suffering of the eunuch at the hands of God's church.

Gregory and Sara

Gregory, a friend who readily identifies with the eunuchs of the Old Testament, recalls years of sexual abuse at the hands of a much older brother as he was growing up. The invasion of Gregory's body by his brother crushed the possibility of normal sexual development for Gregory, begetting sexual addiction that began when Gregory was a teen.[4] In time the shame and self-loathing stemming from his sexual addiction led to other addictions with drugs, alcohol, and food. Gregory went through cycles in which his life spun out of control, followed by seasons of attempts to heal. Eventually, Gregory hit bottom, despairing of his life. Barely able to function, he turned to God for help, committing his life to Christ. With God's help, friends, and therapeutic interventions, Gregory is healing, but the road to shalom has been rocky and slow.

The damage of promiscuity and interlocking addictions in Gregory's life has been staggering, including broken relationships, sexually transmitted infections, unemployment, and more. While today Gregory is a man of deep faith who is recovering well, no one can undo the consequences of his years of acting out. In many ways, he feels that his identity as a Christian man is still limited by the effects of sexual abuse. Because of his sexual history, like the eunuchs in the Pentateuch, he is unwelcome in some churches and could never be ordained or serve in leadership roles in most others. The shame that the church continues to visit upon him hinders his ability to believe in God's full acceptance and love. This in turn hampers his recovery. Though he knows that God is with him and in him, he often suffers the loneliness of a eunuch.

Sara, like Gregory, is a survivor of incest who also became sexually addicted as a young woman. As a result of her promiscuity, Sara repeatedly became pregnant and had several abortions. The physical damage of the abortions left her with numerous gynecological problems requiring surgery later in life. Sara's body carries permanent scars and limitations because of her abuse. She too identifies with the physical and emotional scarring of eunuchs.

While Sara moves deeper into faith and continues to heal from sexual abuse, sometimes she wonders if she will always be single. On hard days she sometimes wonders if God is punishing her by preventing her from finding a loving spouse because of the sins of her past. At such times, she wonders just how much she must be punished before God will be satisfied. Now approaching midlife, she knows that even if God has truly forgiven her, the statistics are against finding a spouse who is emotionally healthy, compatible, and compassionate toward her life history. Sara struggles to come to terms with her past and to trust in the grace of God because of the shaming messages she hears from the church regarding choices she has made in the past. Like Gregory, Sara often feels the alienating pain of the eunuch.

For survivors like Gregory and Sara, the promises of God given explicitly to eunuchs hold forth extraordinary hope. But for this hope to be realized as God desires, the church must repent of its exclusion of "eunuchs" from full participation in the household of God. When God promises to create an everlasting name for faithful, covenant-keeping eunuchs and to give them a powerful place of ministry in God's house of prayer for all people, how can God's church continue to label, judge, and exclude?

A House of Prayer and an Everlasting Name

The first and most foundational promise of this text is that God's heart is open wide to receive and love the eunuch with the same salvation, compassion, and abundance that is offered to anyone who responds to the gift of salvation. God does not label and judge as humans do. God does not have a special category of sexual sin that is unforgivable. (The only sin that cannot be forgiven, according to Jesus, is blasphemy against the Holy Spirit, a form of spiritual pride that haughtily judges and rejects God's gift of salvation.) For the eunuchs who "keep my sabbaths, who choose the things that please me and hold fast my covenant," God promises great reward.

It is important to remember when reading this passage that the command to "keep my sabbaths" is in many ways a command to practice justice and to live a lifestyle of worship. The Sabbath laws of the Old Testament include many elements of economic justice, rest and renewal for aliens and refugees, and proper care of animals and the earth.[5] Sabbath laws are intrinsic to the command to love our neighbor as ourselves. For this reason Isaiah elsewhere preaches that true worship and Sabbath keeping consist of justice for widows, orphans, and others who are at risk (Isa. 58:1–14). It is safe to say that Sabbath is the ongoing practice of worship of the true God that results in actions of justice. These are the very actions that bring about the "great, healing reversals" prophesied by Isaiah. The promise to eunuchs is that if they practice true worship that results in actions of justice, God's favor rests upon them as much as on anyone who lives in this way.

Not only are eunuchs who honor God's covenant welcome with God, but they are also promised a special inheritance that is more powerful than the "normal" legacy of human offspring. "I will give, in my house and within my walls, a monument and a name better than sons and daughters," God says. "I will give them an everlasting name that shall not be cut off" (Isa. 56:5). A few verses later God vows to bring all outcasts (like eunuchs) who trust in the Lord and follow God's ways into God's house, which "will be called a house of prayer for all peoples" (Isa. 56:7–8).

This means that in God's economy, in the great, healing reversals of God's redemption, those who are literally eunuchs and those who typologically identify with the stigma and suffering of eunuchs because of the consequences of sexual abuse, have a uniquely powerful position. A "permanent monument" in God's house refers to perpetual honor and respect in the kingdom of God among the saints, the angels, and the holy Trinity. An "everlasting name that shall not be cut off" refers to spiritual progeny, a heritage of spiritual offspring that will continue to reproduce spiritual children from generation to generation.

These promises are "living and active" words of God to all of us who are in some capacity "eunuchs" because of the consequences of the abuse that we suffered. We can live into these promises, becoming part of God's house of prayer for all people. We can become powerful agents of good news to the outcasts around us, bringing many others into the family of God. Our own experiences of exclusion, shame, self-loathing, and being labeled have given us profound compassion for the suffering of others. Out of our experience of being "eunuchs," we can become dynamic advocates for other eunuchs, indeed for all kinds of people who are pushed to the margins by church and society. Our ministry of intercessory prayer for all people emerges from our journey as eunuchs. Out of that prayer we begin to incarnate the good news that others are longing to hear. We become practitioners of the true Sabbath. This is God's will for us as eunuchs and survivors.

Eros and the Healing of Spiritual Wounds

In order to live into these promises in Isaiah, though, we survivors must choose to heal, a journey of liberation that takes a lifetime. The decision to heal involves daily choices, some of which at the beginning of our journey are very difficult indeed. Without healing from the shame, fear, bitterness, anger, and addictions that are imparted through abuse, we cannot experience the freedom necessary in order to do the wonderful work to which we are called. In particular, our will and our passion, our eros, must be healed so that we can use our inner fire for God's creative, redemptive work.

As Wendy Farley discusses in her extraordinary book *The Wounding and Healing of Desire*, experiences of abuse can keep us captive by distorting our will and our habituated emotional responses to life, with terror, rage, and addiction. Terror is the natural response to being overwhelmed, disempowered, and hurt through sexual abuse. Terror often breeds silence and paralysis. Farley likens the one terrorized to a fawn in the forest. The fawn's only defense mechanism is stillness. Terror paralyzes the survivor's ability to speak, act, and resist injustice in ways that are utterly unconscious:

> The expectation of harm, perhaps even only trivial harm (being embarrassed, evoking someone's ire), becomes so ingrained as a part of consciousness that we do not even notice it. Yet this grid of terror shapes the way we inhabit the world and effects a mutilation of the will. Terror is like gravity: you must accommodate movement to its pull, even though you are hardly aware of it.[6]

Healing from the terror of abuse includes waking up to the ways in which we have been the fawn in the woods. We must regain our ability to act, to speak, and to resist injustice. We must reclaim full moral agency. We have to learn to feel appropriate anger and to channel it in life-giving directions.

In a similar but opposite way, the rage that can result from abuse "eats into various depths in the soul,"[7] enslaving us with its demands and certitude. Unlike the stillness of terror, rage begets habituated responses of aggression. The pilot light is always on, ready to ignite a new, combative fire. Healing from rage requires that we learn to be still when stillness is called for, that we listen before making judgments, and that we come home to the gift of appropriate vulnerability. This reclamation of soul brings about tenderness and humility, along with the authority of a life of clear discernment. The healing of rage enables us to feel and appropriately express righteous anger.

These two responses to abuse—terror and rage—hold many of us survivors hostage for years after our abuse. These two slave masters are behind most of our addictions and our impaired capacity for intimacy.[8] Our capacity to experience divine eros, the energy of desire that leads to healthy vulnerability and self-giving, is crippled by terror and rage.

The healing of terror and rage liberates us so that we can experience the healing of eros—the passion of desire that calls us beyond ourselves to self-giving, creative love. As eros heals, we become able to experience genuine intimacy with God and with other people. This healing process is what enables us fully to become part of God's house of prayer for all people and to become practitioners of God's Sabbath. Without the healing of terror, rage, and addiction, we are unable to discern clearly what is called for in resisting injustice. Without the healing of eros, we lack the creative energy we need to connect with others in healthy ways and to consistently practice justice. To receive the full realization of God's promises to eunuchs, we must cooperate with the Holy Spirit's work in healing us of terror and rage and in restoring our wounded capacity for eros.

Jesus said that to some a gift has been given by God to live as eunuchs for the sake of the kingdom. He made this remarkable statement in the context of a discussion of marriage and discipleship. Jesus himself had this gift. Could it be that in this text Jesus spoke of more than simply choosing not to marry? Could it be that he also had in mind the promises of Isaiah? For what does it mean to be about the kingdom of God if it is not to gather the outcasts, live in Sabbath rest, and proclaim the year of the Lord's favor? The Word of the Lord to all us eunuchs is a word of healing and hope. It is time for the church to hear this word and to repent of her exclusion of the least of these.

For Reflection

For Survivors

1. Which of the great, healing reversals of Isaiah speak personally to you, and why?
2. Describe a time when you witnessed or experienced someone being ridiculed or excluded because of their sexual ambiguity.
3. When I read that God has special promises just for eunuchs, and that those who have suffered sexual abuse are a type of eunuch:
   a. I feel . . .
   b. I imagine . . .
   c. I wonder . . .
   d. I pray . . .

For Those Who Journey with Us

1. Which of the great, healing reversals of Isaiah speak personally to you, and why?

2. Describe a time when you witnessed or experienced someone being ridiculed or excluded because of their sexual ambiguity.
3. What are some ways the church could be invited to reflect upon the promises of God to eunuchs in Isaiah? What are the obstacles to opening the church's eyes to these promises for eunuchs?
4. When I read that God has special promises just for eunuchs, and that those who have suffered sexual abuse are a type of eunuch:
   a. I feel . . .
   b. I imagine . . .
   c. I wonder . . .
   d. I pray . . .

Recommended Activities

- Watch: *Billy Elliot*
- Create: Bake a large batch of homemade bread, working the dough with your hands rather than a bread machine. (Plenty of good recipes are available on the internet.) As you knead the dough, meditate on God's promises to those who are eunuchs, those who will have a lasting memorial in God's house. When the bread is finished, share it with a neighbor or friend as a sign of the abundance of creative self-giving that is possible through the healing of eros.
- Read: *The Wounding and Healing of Desire* by Wendy Farley

9

We Are Clean

The maple leaves outside my window danced in the autumn breeze like a thousand red ballerinas, while a wedge of Canada Geese honked their way south. Shafts of sunlight reached across my desk in a long handprint of blessing. A tentative knock let me know Carrie had arrived. She paused in the doorway, hesitant. "Pastor," she said, "this is going to be really hard. I don't know if I can do it."

"Carrie," I replied, "you don't have to tell me your story until you feel ready, and if you never feel ready, it will be okay. I will still be glad to know you and you will still be welcome here in our church." I motioned her toward the sitting area with its old wingback chairs while I poured two cups of coffee.

"No," she insisted, "I just have to do this. When I met you at the retreat and I heard everyone sharing, I knew that I had to come and see you and tell you everything I ever did wrong. I want to be a Christian, but I have to tell you everything. I am a sinner." She sat in the chair across from me and grabbed the box of tissue from the table, embracing it with both arms. I wondered about her previous spiritual formation that made her feel she had to confess to me, the pastor, "everything she ever did wrong" in order to be accepted by God. I consciously relaxed my posture even more, silently praying for the Holy Spirit to bring peace and to help Carrie know she was in a safe space.

Swallowing hard and taking one of the tissues from the box, Carrie began. "I've been clean from crack for three months," she said, watching me closely to see how I would respond. I continued to listen, nodding gently. Carrie continued, "I've done so many bad things in my life. I am so ashamed." Her eyes filled with tears.

"It is okay to stop whenever you want to," I said. She needed a few moments to regain composure. I continued, "Carrie, your story is sacred, because God has been with you, loving you through every moment of your life. No matter what mistakes you have made or sins you have committed, God has been there loving you and is bringing you into freedom now because he loves you." Tears streamed down Carrie's face.

"I can feel that love, Pastor," she said. "That's what makes me want to tell you everything." Over the next hour the tiny wisp of a woman with strange hair and a pierced lip described a lifetime of addictions, abuse, promiscuity, divorce, suffering, scrapes with the police, and poverty. Every relationship in her life had been shattered by addictions and abuse. Her body had aged because of the drugs and hard times so that she looked older than her years. Her voice was husky from cigarettes and booze. Each time she shared another story she ended with, "That was easier than I thought it would be. This isn't nearly as hard as I thought it would be." I listened.

Finally Carrie stopped talking. She looked at me and said, "That's it. That's everything. I can't believe I didn't use this whole box of tissue. Pastor, I have been a bad, bad person. Am I still welcome here?"

This was the beginning of Carrie's healing, a transformation that very slowly rippled from the inside out, touching all aspects of her existence and gradually spilling into her family and friends. Carrie continues to heal today, in the company of Christian friends. When she stumbles, which is often, they help her. When they are hurting, she helps them. Carrie is like the woman who wept on Jesus's feet and kissed them and wiped them with her hair (Luke 7:36–50). She loves much because she has been forgiven much. Every scar that Carrie bears is becoming a source of compassion and healing for others.

I have known other Carries along the way—prostitutes, drug addicts, alcoholics, sex addicts, people who cut themselves, burn themselves, and survive suicide attempts. Of all the people with whom I have journeyed in healing, these are the ones whose transformation touches me the most. Healing is often slow and halting, a "two steps forward and one step back" struggle. Their deliverance from chaos takes time, with many failures along the way. Those who make it into freedom do so because they have been welcomed into the journey by Christian friends. That is, while therapy helps, the most important ingredient in their recovery is friendship. Which raises many questions for us in the church today.

A Friend of Sinners

"Jesus, what a friend for sinners," the old hymn says, and we sing it with gusto on Sunday morning in our pews. But would we really like Jesus if he showed up and was the "friend of sinners" among us that he was two thousand years ago? Could we relate? Imagine Jesus coming to earth today in Dallas, Texas. He would drive an old pickup, wear jeans, and drink beer. The Dallas Jesus would not live in Park Cities. He would live in Oak Cliff or south Garland and drive to Park Cities to take care of other people's lawns or put new roofs on their houses. He would have the kind of job that meant showering at the end of the day rather than in the morning.

There would be thick calluses on his hands. When the Dallas Jesus shopped at Wal-Mart, the person at the door would always check his bag against his receipt while letting the Anglos pass by, because his skin would be the color of molasses. For that same reason the Dallas Jesus would be pulled over by the police sometimes when he had done nothing wrong.

The Dallas Jesus would have many friends with problems, many Carries in his life and neighborhood. The people down at the county jail would know him by name, because he would be there on his day off to visit friends. Jesus would be a favorite at neighborhood parties, the kind where liquor flows freely and one-night stands begin, because he would know, and love, and want to be with his neighbors, right in the middle of their lives. And they would love him back.

Would the Dallas Jesus and his friends be welcome in the church? Would he even be *recognized*?

Three stories in the Gospels sum up how we survivors see Jesus, the friend of sinners. They are found back-to-back in Mark and Luke, and with some other stories between them in Matthew. In many ways, this narrative trio tells the whole story of the aftermath of sexual abuse, although it is never explicitly named as such in the gospels. Even more importantly, these three stories tell survivors how Jesus sees us in every possible manifestation of our pain—the consequences of having been sinned against and then of having become sinful ourselves—and what Jesus is willing to do to heal our pain. These are the stories of a Gerasene man, a bleeding woman, and a twelve-year-old girl.

Unclean

In our tidy American culture, we think of "clean and unclean" in terms of soaps and showers and hand sanitizers. We think of a cluttered house that needs attention, or a dirty car. But in Jesus's culture being unclean resulted in exile. For various degrees of contamination people had to stay separate from family, friends, and congregation until the proper cleansing rituals had taken place and the priest had given permission to return to normal life. Being unclean had physical, spiritual, relational, and communal dimensions. People became unclean through illness, bleeding, menstruation, bodily discharges, coming into contact with another unclean person, touching a corpse, or eating food that was not kosher. These are just a few examples. The origins of the "clean and unclean" laws go back to the exodus experience, when God gave the Law to help the Hebrew people form an identity that was distinct from all the surrounding oppressive cultures that did not honor Yahweh.[1] The following three stories are about a man, a woman, and a child who are unclean, and what Jesus does to set them free.

Legion

Everything about the Gerasene man is unclean.[2] He lives in the tombs, the place of the dead. He has become so uncontrollable in his anguish that he can no longer be among the living. His violent outbursts have made him a danger to society. They try containing him with chains and shackles and guards, but even those are no match for his terrible rage. Tearing away the chains and his clothes, the man rushes into the wild, driven by demons. He has been living in the tombs, naked, for a long time. Whatever happened to him before we meet him has filled him with shame and loathing and a compulsion to expose his body.

Outside the cemetery his neighbors raise swine, the ultimate unclean animal in Jewish culture. When Jesus arrives at the shore near the cemetery, the man rushes toward him, driven by the army[3] of unclean spirits. Luke writes, "When he saw Jesus, he fell down before him and shouted at the top of his voice, 'What have you to do with me, Jesus, Son

of the Most High God? I beg you, do not torment me'"
(Luke 8:28).

The man longs to be whole. He rushes *toward* Jesus. Yet
the demonic forces that harass him fear Jesus and want to run
away. They recognize his authority. They are frantic, frenzied,
willing to do anything to get away from Jesus, even be sent
into a herd of swine. The man is torn apart by these conflicting forces—a desire to be whole and a desire to self-destruct.
Moved with compassion, Jesus delivers and heals the man
from the demonic oppression. The unclean spirits rush into
a herd of swine, sending them into a frenzy so that the swine
plunge over a cliff into the water where they drown.

Some of us survivors see in the Gerasene man our own
story of redemption. We were driven by dark forces that had
rendered our existence a living death. We were fragmented
into a confusion of pain and need and sin. We became "other"
to everything that is "normal" in our culture. We were hos-
tile to the church, at war with society, disintegrated within
ourselves. We were outcasts from our family and friends. As
we looked around, it seemed to us that even animals were
more sane and at peace than we were.

In our profound state of "uncleanness," we were the least
of these. Jesus crossed the lake to the other side, our side,
just for us. And now we are "clothed and in our right minds,"
going among our people with the good news of what God
has done. Jesus wants our people to see that we are clean.

Twelve Years

A crowd is waiting to meet Jesus when he returns from the
Gerasenes. Among them is Jairus, an important leader in the
synagogue. He is desperate because his only child, a twelve-
year-old daughter, is dying. As Jesus slowly moves toward the
house of Jairus, another story begins to unfold. An unclean
woman presses in. She has been bleeding for twelve long years.

Her gynecological condition has rendered her unclean, making her life a barren wasteland of pain, suffering, exclusion, and judgment from the people around her. Because of her sexual wound, she has been banned from worship and from touching others, even members of her family. Every relationship in her life has suffered. She has spent all her money on physicians, who, according to Mark's account, have inflicted even more suffering upon her so that she has grown worse (Mark 5:25–26). This bleeding, unclean woman gathers all her courage and moves into the crowd. She inches her way along until finally she is able to lean forward, her fingers brushing the hem of Jesus's clothes. She is behind him where she is sure he will not notice the touch. No one will know, she thinks. But maybe the healing power will fall upon her as it has on others.

The moment she touches Jesus the bleeding stops. So does the procession. "Who touched me?" Jesus asks, to the amazement of his disciples. They try to tell him his question does not make sense. But Jesus will not let it go. "Someone touched me," he says, "for I noticed that power had gone out from me" (Luke 8:45). Then in the middle of the crowd with the whole town watching, Jesus pronounces the liberating words, "Daughter, your faith has made you well; go in peace" (Luke 8:48). With those words Jesus uncurses this daughter of God from twelve long years of suffering from brokenness at the center of her sexuality.

This is the story of survivors whose bodies and souls bleed in a thousand different ways, whose emotional, financial, and familial resources drain away year by year while our suffering only grows worse. It is the story of survivors who live in a barren wilderness of chronic, low-grade depression, who go from doctor to doctor to try to understand the nightmares, the phobias, the anxiety, the gynecological problems, the pain, only to be labeled and judged and medicated with treatments that do not bring healing. It is the story of daughters of God who have almost come to believe that we are our condition.

Almost. Deeper than that, it is the story of our holy subversion, our decision to touch Jesus even if the whole town blocks our way. This is the story of our healing. We were the least of these, unclean from twelve long years of bleeding, and Jesus made us whole.

There is one last event in this trio of stories about uncleanness, and it too is a narrative of twelve years. But this time, the one suffering is a little girl. The Bible does not tell us what happened to the unnamed child, only that at twelve years of age she began to die (Luke 8:42). As she entered puberty her life drained away.

Mary Pipher describes the draining of adolescent girls' lives in *Reviving Ophelia*, her landmark work on the epidemic loss of selfhood that girls experience in US American society upon entering adolescence.[4] She calls girls "saplings in the storm" because of the many forces arrayed against them as they move from the freedom and adventure of childhood through puberty into a world where they will be judged on their sexual appeal. Even for girls from strong families where, like Jairus's daughter, they are dearly loved, girls in our culture are at risk.

Twelve years of age, the symbolic age of puberty, is the threshold where far too many girls split into a false self, one that is determined by the sexually abusive culture of our day.[5] Pressured to deny most of their gifts and abilities, faced with an adult future determined by sexism and many other dehumanizing "isms," many girls slide into a long, slow depression in which they increasingly distort and deny their own selfhood. Out of that pain emerges many forms of self-injury—anorexia, bulimia, and cutting, to name a few. Like the twelve-year-old daughter of Jairus, their life drains away at the very time God intended them to thrive into full-grown women.

Into the midst of this slow death, Jesus strides. He is unwilling to accept the verdict of the crowd. "Child, get up!" he cries, taking her by the hand. And through his body, the church, Jesus longs to take the hand of every dying girl and give back to her the life that God intends.

Whether the wounds of sexual abuse came through pornographic, misogynistic culture, draining our lives away one day at a time, or through violence at the hands of family members, coaches, or priests, we survivors read the healing stories of Luke 8 with a different set of lenses. In these stories we see the consequences of our abuse played out in a lifetime of suffering. We see the isolation, the labeling, the exclusion, and the sin. But larger than all the wounds we see redemption. For the same Jesus who got into a boat and crossed over to the other side, the same Jesus who called a bleeding woman "daughter," the same Jesus who said, "*Talitha cum*! Little girl, arise!" has come to us. He has given back our lives. And we will never agree to participate in our own subjugation again. Christ has set us free.

For Reflection

For Survivors

1. In what ways have you experienced conflicting desires to be healed and to run away from healing?
2. How have you experienced Jesus saying *talitha cum* to you?
3. As I read about the woman who bled for twelve long years:
   a. I thought . . .
   b. I felt . . .
   c. I remembered . . .
   d. I wished . . .
   e. I prayed . . .

For Those Who Journey with Us

1. What would it mean for you to "get in the boat and cross over to the other side"? What would be the challenges? What would be the risks?
2. As I read about the woman who bled for twelve long years:

a. I thought . . .
b. I felt . . .
c. I remembered . . .
d. I wished . . .
e. I prayed . . .

Recommended Activities

- Watch: *Whale Rider*; *Reign Over Me*; *Juno*; *Girl, Interrupted*
- Create: Complete a series of paintings or drawings that tell the story of the healing of the Gerasene man.
- Read: *Reviving Ophelia* by Mary Pipher

10

About Judas and Mary

Six days before Passover, John tells us, Jesus went to Bethany, to the house of Lazarus, whom he had raised from the dead (John 12:1–11). A party was under way, with Jesus as the guest of honor. There he was enjoying a dish that Martha had prepared, when a woman came into the room. Mary. Something about the look on her face made everyone pause. What was that in her hands? It looked like an alabaster jar. What was she doing? Kneeling at Jesus's feet, Mary broke the thin neck of the jar. Aromatic waves of nard filled the room. Silence.

Everyone knew that fragrance. It was the ointment used for embalming. Nard was the bittersweet smell of grief. Tenderly, Mary lavished upon Jesus's feet a gift that had cost a full year's wages. Releasing her hair from its bonds, Mary bent low and with it began to wipe Jesus's feet. Tears mingled with oil, the disciple's sorrow and devotion spilling down onto the floor. Everyone stared, appalled. A woman touching a man who was not her husband? A scandalous act of intimacy. Yet it was not sexual. It was something else. She used nard.

A voice shattered the silence. "Why was this perfume not sold for three hundred denarii and the money given to the poor?" Judas demanded (John 12:5).

John tells us that Judas cared nothing for the poor. He used their suffering as a cover for his sin. He was a man hungry for money, freely helping himself to the common purse. We do not know how Judas fell into bondage with mammon. We only know that he was willing to sell the Son of God for a handful of coins. He was a man filled with craving and frustration. Jesus was not the Messiah that Judas thought he should be. And we know that Jesus knew this, long before the night of his arrest.

In a moment of exquisite beauty, the prophecy of nard wafting in the air, Judas trampled the heart of worship with his words. This is a scene that is familiar to survivors, for there is often a Judas at our shoulder, shouting and judging the freedom in our lives. Judas does not see our sanctity, nor does he respect our gifts. The spirit of Judas is one of contempt and exploitation. It relegates women to subservience and children to the margins. It forms alliances with principalities and powers. Judas uses people to build self-serving empires in the name of God. For Judas everything in life is reducible to money and control, but these are couched in pious talk. The real kingdom of God is an offense.

The spirit of Judas is why many of us find ourselves outside the gates of the church. We will not submit to Judas. As many feminists and womanists have said, there is a link between racism, sexism, abuse of all kinds, and an empire-building church. The principality that drives pogroms and lynchings and rapes is bound to the spirit of Judas. Inquisitions, witch hunts, and character assassinations of holy men and women are driven by the spirit of Judas. There is nothing more insidious or more resistant to exorcism than this spirit of Judas. It utterly despises the likes of Mary.

But when Judas judges her, the voice of Jesus warns, "Leave. Her. Alone."

As we heal, a great many of us survivors become like Mary. We have opened our alabaster jars. Our lives are spilled in ministry to Christ. We are free in our worship; we are outrageous. Our hair tumbles down as we kneel at Jesus's feet. The grief of our lives has become anointing oil. Jesus receives our love with open arms. But to Judas we are objects of contempt.

Juan and Karen

Juan came to my office on a chilly winter day. A part-time construction worker, he was stocky and of average height, with gray just beginning to appear at his temples. A divorced father of two, Juan was a survivor of incest. His healing was well under way the day we talked about his Judas. Now on the staff of a medium-sized, mainline church, Juan was responsible for spiritual formation ministries. He worked part time for the church, supplementing his income with construction projects.

Because of his experiences of healing from sexual abuse, Juan had become a "Mary," a contemplative of great depth and discernment. While going through seminary, Juan had discovered the Christian mystics and in them found kindred spirits. He was especially drawn to Brother Lawrence of the Resurrection. The "practice of the presence of God" through the ordinary events of daily life had helped to heal the grief Juan carried from his childhood. Ignatian practices of prayer had also brought much freedom and peace to Juan, as he learned to pray with Scripture using the ancient method of *lectio divina*.

Because of his depth of prayer and discernment, Juan became a sought-after spiritual advisor in his congregation. Many people were drawn to the beauty and holiness of his life. He was especially gifted in companioning young adults. With Juan they were able to explore questions of vocation and find their own voice as they moved from adolescence to adult-

113

hood. Because of his own vocational journey and the role his healing had played in his spiritual development, Juan was an exceptionally compassionate and nonjudgmental pastor.

As Juan became more influential within the congregation, another pastor on staff became jealous. She began to look for ways to undermine Juan's pastoral authority, speaking disrespectfully about him to others and at times humiliating him in staff meetings. Juan should spend more time in the office, she said. He was not accountable enough for how he used his time. Juan had been seen in a pub with a group of young adults, talking about the Bible. The pub was no place for Christians or the Bible, she complained. The church's reputation would be tarnished.

Gradually, the other pastor gained a small but powerful following among congregants who wielded financial control in the church. When Juan came to see me, he was in great distress. Not only was the church being divided into factions by the other pastor, but Juan's ordination process was now in danger as well. The other pastor was using her political connections in the denomination to make life hard for him. Juan had met the religious spirit of Judas.

Karen, like Juan, was a contemplative. She had grown up in a very conservative evangelical church. In her early twenties, Karen had been attacked and raped by two men who were known to her through her father's business. For years she had told no one of her trauma. Using the only theological resources at her disposal—the Bible and prayer—Karen prayed her grief and searched her Bible for answers. Therapy was not an option for her in her tradition. Over a long period of time, Karen experienced healing through meditative prayer and Scripture. Out of her suffering, Karen found her way onto the contemplative path. Karen's Bible-college training had done little to expose her to contemplative Christian traditions, but years later she discovered Julian of Norwich and several other Christian mystics. Just as Juan had done, Karen experienced kinship with the spirituality of these saints. Their writing affirmed her experiences of healing prayer. Karen's prayer life demonstrated extraordinary depth and power.

Out of her experiences, Karen became a gifted spiritual companion for others who had suffered abuse. By the time I met her, Karen was middle-aged and had encountered the spirit of Judas several times. As an evangelical, Karen moved in circles where people were routinely taught from the pulpit that women should keep silence in the church and that women should submit to their husbands, who were the spiritual head of their homes. In her denomination, women were defined exclusively by roles of wife and mother. Many of the women who came to Karen for spiritual guidance were single, divorced, widowed, childless, or in relationships with abusive men. They felt invisible and disempowered in their church and unable to resolve the grief in their lives. Karen helped them to find their identity in Christ rather than in socially constructed gender roles.

"Are we really just a collection of breasts and wombs?" Karen would ask in women's retreats. "Is a woman still beautiful and precious if her breasts are lost through cancer or her womb is gone because of a hysterectomy? What if we are unable to have children, or God does not call us to marriage? What if our children are grown and gone? Do we no longer count? Are we really only worth our sexual functions?" Karen dared to ask the questions that were not allowed in her denomination. "Jesus doesn't define us by sexuality," Karen said, pointing to Mark 3:35. "He calls us his sisters and mothers and brothers if we do the will of God."

Karen was a Mary, and she called forth other survivors to walk the contemplative path so that they became free in Christ too. Karen suffered much at the hands of Judas in the church, with slander, accusations, and exclusion. Yet she continued faithfully in ministry to Jesus, as did Juan, and she remains in her conservative tradition. Juan's ordination eventually went through but only with much struggle.

Long after Karen and Juan are gone, their ministries will continue to bear fruit through others. Like Mary, they have been given a legacy in the kingdom that no one can take away. Yet we must ask ourselves, why do we allow the church to continue to wound and reject Karen, Juan, and thousands of other Marys whose gifts are what the church needs the most? Why do we reward Judas and scoff at Mary?

Becoming Mary

The contemplative way, the way of Mary, can seem foolish at first glance. For contemplatives, being has primacy over doing. Action proceeds from listening and being, and in the best case, one's being is steeped in God's love. In an often-quoted story, Jesus praised Mary over Martha because Martha's "doing" orientation led her to fragmentation. Mary had chosen "the one thing necessary," the contemplative posture of being and listening (Luke 10:43). Mary's orientation is one of openness, vulnerability, availability, and grace. Being Mary requires child-like trust in the goodness of the Lord, even when the way is hard and lonely. Contemplatives "waste" much time at the feet of Jesus, learning to recognize the movements of the Spirit. Prayer is what keeps the Marys right side up. "My sheep hear my voice," Jesus says in John 10, and contemplatives believe him. Marys have chosen to live as if Jesus speaks the truth.

That is why we are free.[1] Jesus says that his Word has made us clean, and we believe it (John 15:3). His Word is changing the way we think about ourselves. When the voice of Judas tries to re-instill messages of shame, the Word of Jesus washes it away. We hear Jesus saying to us instead, "You are chosen and beloved." When Judas tries to stop us from living our vocation, Jesus comes near. "Be of good courage," he whispers, "I have overcome the world" (John 16:33). When we feel overwhelmed by memories of our abuse, Jesus reminds us that he was there with us, the least of these. This empowers

116

us to move away from thinking of ourselves as victims and to move toward reclaiming full agency in our own lives. We are strengthened by the knowledge that Jesus has risen from the dead and that his resurrection power is now within us, raising us to new life. The contemplative path, the way of Mary, is one in which we are cleansed and made whole by listening to the voice of Jesus. In this way the voice of Judas loses its power over us. No matter what happens, we know we belong to Christ. Judas cannot take that away.

"Behold, I make all things new," Jesus says, and for us this is the best news of all (Rev. 21:5). Through these words Jesus gives us "beauty for ashes, the oil of joy for mourning, and a garment of praise for the spirit of despair" (Isa. 61:3). As we meditate on these words, we come to believe, as did Julian of Norwich, that when Jesus heals our wounds we are even more beautiful than we would have been if we had never been broken. Out of this assurance comes a clarity that protects our hearts from the judgments and rage of Judas.

What we are experiencing in our own lives could help to heal the rest of God's church, for the body of Christ suffers much from Judas. Wherever there is a thirst for power, a quest for money, an obsession with status in the church, we may be sure that the spirit of Judas is at work. Powers and principalities infest the systems of the church when the spirit of Judas has sway, distorting spiritual discipline into legalism, twisting mercy into judgment, and reversing Galatians 3:26–28 so that God's people are fractured by gender, race, and class.

So we reach out to you, sisters and brothers, to all who are weary, all whose hearts have been broken by the world and by the spirit of Judas in the church. Come with us to Jesus. Let us kneel at his feet and anoint him with our molten grief. Our tears and our memories, our longings are welcome there. Judas cannot come into that space. As we empty our sighs and wordless prayers, love will set us free. Out of this love and freedom comes the power to resist the spirit of Judas for the sake of God's church and God's world.

For Reflection

For Survivors

1. The scene with Mary crossing the room and kneeling at Jesus's feet reminds me of . . .
2. I have encountered the spirit of Judas in . . .
3. When I think about Jesus telling Judas to leave Mary alone:
   a. I think . . .
   b. I feel . . .
   c. I wonder . . .
   d. I pray . . .

For Those Who Journey with Us

1. The scene with Mary crossing the room and kneeling at Jesus's feet reminds me of . . .
2. I have encountered the spirit of Judas in . . .
3. When I think about Jesus telling Judas to leave Mary alone:
   a. I think . . .
   b. I feel . . .

c. I wonder . . .

d. I pray . . .

4. As leaders of God's church, how can we guard against becoming "infected" with the spirit of Judas?

Recommended Activities

- Feel: Make an appointment to have a foot massage. As the massage therapist applies the fragrant oil to your feet, imagine the comfort Jesus felt at Mary's nurturing, safe touch. Allow this experience to be a form of prayer, connecting you with Jesus's love for Mary and with her offering of nurturing, safe touch to Jesus.

- Create: Draw, paint, sculpt, or photograph an image representing Mary anointing Jesus's feet and wiping them with her hair.

- Discover: Using a good Bible dictionary, find out more about life in Jesus's day. Read about denarii, burial customs, nard, and cultural norms regarding prohibitions against unmarried women and men touching one another.

11

Emmanuel

Emmanuel, the special name for Jesus that we sing about at Christmastime, means "God with us." Emmanuel is God incarnate, God coming to live with all the struggles that mark our lives, *God as the least of these.* From conception to death, Jesus lived in solidarity with our hunger, our suffering, and our need. Survivors read the story of Jesus with an eye for all the ways he suffered.

Jesus and his family were poor. His cradle was a feed trough. His parents offered two doves for the temple sacrifice, the offering that poor people used (Luke 2:22–24). When Jesus was a baby, his family fled to Egypt as political refugees hiding from a bloody tyrant (Matt. 2:15–23). Like refugees today, they watched and waited, wondering when it would be safe to go home. At his baptism as a young man, the Holy Spirit descended as a dove, the sacrificial animal of the poor (Luke 3:21–22). During his final years of life, Jesus was essentially homeless, dependent on the hospitality of others. As he walked the dusty roads teaching, preaching, and healing, Jesus stayed with friends. He told would-be disciples, "Foxes have holes and birds have their nests, but the Son of Man has nowhere to lay his head" (Luke 9:58). Jesus rode in borrowed boats and sat on a borrowed donkey. When he died he was buried in a borrowed tomb.

Emmanuel, God with us, willingly identified with the poor—the working poor, the devastatingly poor, the homeless, the displaced. We survivors read the Gospels and see that Jesus knows firsthand the poverty we face when we flee abusive relationships only to find ourselves and our children homeless, with nothing but the clothes on our backs. We recognize in Emmanuel the face of every refugee longing for home, living in squalor, haunted with memories of violence.

The friend of sinners, Jesus enraged the authorities by exposing their exploitive and unloving ways. His virtue revealed their vice. From the beginning of his ministry, they plotted to kill him because they couldn't bear the truth that he spoke. At last their day came, and they bound him and beat him, mocked him and took him away. Emmanuel is God with us survivors who are punished for telling the truth. Our perpetrators were pastors, priests, coaches, Boy Scout leaders, and parents. The empire we resisted was church, school, and community. We told the truth and were shamed and humiliated while our offenders went free. We were shunned by our neighbors who said there was no way Pastor could have done those things or asked who we thought we were to tell such lies. Our stories were swept under the church rug while our offender was quietly assigned to another parish. We were lambs at the mercy of wolves, and the Lamb of God was with us, walking to Golgotha.

Oh, the deep, deep love that binds Jesus to us! Jesus is unwilling to separate himself from anything that we suffer. Jesus chose to experience even the pain of our sexual abuse. We know this because he was sexually abused as his life drained away.

Jesus a Victim of Sexual Abuse

I never heard a pastor preach about this in all my years in the church. Nor did I hear a professor talk about it when I went through graduate theological education. I have come to realize that the reason Jesus's sexual abuse has not been named is that we survivors were not the ones doing the theology, at least not from our perspective as survivors. Our voices *as* the least of these were not considered official or important in the formulation of Christology, soteriology, hamartiology, pneumatology, and all the other "ologies" within theology.[1] On the contrary, we were not credible precisely because of our femaleness, our woundedness, our sexuality, our bodiliness, our "otherness." The idea that we might know something about God that other people missed because of our otherness was an offense. Who did we think we were, anyway?

But thanks be to God we are in a new day. We are finding our voices in the academy and the church, and we have much to say.

Jesus Suffers with Us

None of us sees images or sculptures of Jesus naked in the church. Religious art always shows him with a loincloth. But Jesus was crucified naked. Being stripped publicly prior to his crucifixion was a calculated act of sexual violence. In Jesus's culture, as in Middle Eastern cultures today, to be stripped naked in front of a watching crowd was an act of sexual violation. Witness the dreadful images coming out of Abu Ghraib prison.

The torture was sadistic, carried out while he was naked in order to maximize his humiliation in front of the voyeuristic crowd. Like a child victim of rape or a victim in snuff porn, Jesus was pinned down, bound, violated, penetrated, torn. He was displayed as a naked object of contempt while the blood poured from his broken body. Jesus died in this position while his perpetrators played games with his stolen clothing. Mary stood by powerless to stop the blasphemous crime. She and the other women were like thousands of men, women, and children today who are forced to watch their loved ones tortured, raped, mutilated, and murdered by the armies of despotic leaders. Like those victims of violence, Jesus died in the dark night of his abuse.

Christa

Usually art is more powerful than words to communicate a spiritual truth. Edwina Sandys's sculpture of Christ on the cross as a woman, Christa, was installed in New York's Cathedral of St. John the Divine in 1984. After only eleven days Christa was removed. Her presence was "indefensible" to critics, including a bishop of the church.[2] For most of the last twenty years, Christa was stored away from public view.

Christa is controversial precisely because she links Jesus's crucifixion with the sexual abuse of women. Critics believe that the portrayal of Jesus as a woman who is naked and experiencing abuse blasphemes the Lord. These critics have no problem with Jesus being mostly naked on a cross as long as he remains male. Presenting him as female suddenly turns the crucifix from a meditation on Emmanuel, God with us, into pornography. The inability of critics to make the obvious connection between Jesus, Christa, and the suffering of millions of women and girls boggles the mind. Yet it is only one example of the loss of conscience of the church in regard to the sanctity of female life. It is just one more outcome of patriarchy.

As Marie Fortune notes, Christa appears pornographic to many viewers because our culture is saturated with images of sexual violence against women, and these images are produced for entertainment.[3] Television programs such as CSI are wildly popular in no small part because of their frequent sadomasochistic sexual themes.[4] Because of the pervasiveness of such images, many Christians are unable to see Edwina Sandys's Christa as Jesus's solidarity with the suffering of victims of sexual abuse. Ironically, they can see that to subject Jesus to sexual abuse would be blasphemous, yet they see nothing inherently blasphemous in the often sexually violent themes of CSI. This disconnect betrays a poverty of official theology at many levels, not least of which is the meaning of the doctrine of atonement, an issue to which we will now turn our attention. For if the whole point of Jesus's incarnation is his death to pay an angry God the blood debt for guilty sinners, his solidarity with "the least of these" in all aspects of embodied life disappears. His life becomes one more story of the inexplicable, unconscionable violence of a demonic parent against a vulnerable child.

Atonement and the Least of These

Atonement is a theological concept that explains how broken, sinful people are brought back into one accord (at-one-ment) with God. All theories of atonement (and there are several) contain inherent presuppositions about the nature of sin, how people become sinful, how sin affects the world, and how God views sin. Atonement theory, as you can see, is closely tied to hamartiology, or the study of sin. It is also bound to soteriology, the study of salvation. What does atonement theory look like when we understand that Jesus is Emmanuel, God with us, *as* the least of these? What does *that* theory of atonement mean for survivors?

First it means that in his public execution before a jeering crowd, Jesus experienced exactly the kind of objectification that is inflicted upon women, men, and children whose naked bodies are broken for the sexual entertainment of others. Through the cross, Emmanuel, God with us, took into his own body and spirit the humiliation and the agony of our sexual abuse. Jesus carried the shame of every victim's cross—those

125

of us who survived and those who didn't—to his own cross, disarming the "rulers and authorities," the arbiters of shame, so that they no longer have the power to define us (Col. 2:9–15).

Atonement for us survivors means that through the power of Jesus's resurrection, we are no longer doomed to live out the broken consequences of the abuse. Because the Holy Spirit is counseling us and comforting us, teaching us about Jesus's healing love, we do not have to keep repeating the patterns of wounds and sin and grief. We can have at-one-ment with Christ, who heals us and sets us free. Yet for the good news of this healing to be made clear, we must resist all theories of atonement that are punitive, that place Jesus in the hands of an angry, vindictive God.

One of the primary reasons the good news of the gospel has seemed like bad news to survivors of sexual abuse is that we have been led to believe that the theory of penal substitutionary atonement is what the gospel is about. Penal substitutionary atonement is the concept that all humans deserve to suffer eternally in hell in conscious torment because we have sinned against God. In this theory, Jesus came to earth, suffered, and died on the cross primarily to take the punishment that we deserve from God the Father. In other words, every man, woman, and child ever born "deserves to be crucified" because we have offended God so much. But Jesus stepped in and took the punishment as a substitute for us and thereby paid the debt we owe. According to this model, God pours out his wrath against humanity's sin upon Jesus. Jesus stands between a guilty humanity and a just God, paying the debt of sin. This theory of atonement is "penal" because it is focused on punishment for lawbreaking.

Molly

When I went into my office, the light on my telephone was flashing, notifying me of voice mail. There was just one message this time. It was from Molly, one of my students. She had been out of class for three weeks. A quiet young woman, Molly usually sat toward the back of the room. She was tiny, scarcely larger than a child, with long red curls that fell below her shoulders. Her green eyes were almond shaped, giving her an elfin beauty. Even though the semester was more than half over, I felt like I did not know Molly, because she rarely spoke in class.

"Dr. Heath, I was in the hospital for a while. I'm sorry I missed class. I need to ask for an incomplete so I can finish my work. I'll try to catch you on campus this week."

The next day Molly appeared at my office door.

"Oh, Molly! I am glad to see you. I got your message. I hope you are feeling better," I said, gesturing to a chair. She came in and sat down.

"Well, let's just say I'm in a better space. Safer, probably." There was a pause.

"Dr. Heath, I'm being treated for depression." She watched my face to see how I would respond. A safer space? She had been in the hospital for depression. Had Molly been thinking of hurting herself? I kept my voice calm.

"Well, Molly, the most important thing is to take good care of yourself, and it sounds like you made a wise choice to get some help. An incomplete is no big deal. You're a fine student, and I'm sure you'll be able to catch up."

"Dr. Heath, can I ask you something?" she said. She perched on the edge of the chair, her manner reminding me of a frightened bird.

"Sure," I answered, moving around from behind my desk to my wingback chair under the window. "Let me just move over here where it's a little more comfortable. Would you like some coffee or tea?" I had a feeling she might need to talk for a while.

"No thanks. It's kind of hard to talk about, but I have to ask you." Her voice tightened with fear.

"I'm listening, Molly. Just take your time."

"Well, it's about God. And sin." She paused again, summoning the courage to say what would come next. "The thing is, well, I'm just going to say it. When I was eighteen I had an abortion." Her voice stopped abruptly, as if the words had broken free of their own accord, leaving her in shock. I waited. Molly's voice trembled. Her hands twisted the corner of her scarf into a knot. While she spoke she stared at the floor. "I was pregnant because I got raped. They warned us about date rape in high school. I never thought it would happen to me." She glanced up, her eyes filled with pain, then dropped her gaze to the floor again. "It's against my religion to have an abortion. I knew it was wrong, but I didn't know what to do and I was so afraid. I never told my parents. They still don't know. They would kill me if they knew. But I just couldn't have a baby from rape." Tears ran down her cheeks. She brushed them away with the edge of her scarf. I handed her a box of tissues.

"Oh, Molly, I am so sorry. That must have been so incredibly painful. You must have felt so alone making your decision." I waited while she wept for a moment.

"Yes, alone. Dr. Heath, do you think I'm going to hell? Do you think God will ever forgive me? I've told him over and over I'm sorry, but I never feel forgiven. All I feel is God's wrath. My church teaches that if you have an abortion you are definitely going to hell. My parents believe that too. I feel so ashamed. I feel filthy. I know this is why I get so depressed. It's God's punishment. Sometimes I just want to die." Her voice broke into deep, keening sobs of utter despair.

When she regained composure, Molly explained how she had been taught a punitive model of atonement from as far back as she could remember. As a young girl in Sunday school, she remembered seeing pictures of Jesus on the cross and hearing the teacher say that God was punishing Jesus for everyone else's sin, because God was angry at sin. Combined with a deeply embedded image of God as wrathful Judge,

Molly learned that sexual sin was especially loathsome to God. She blamed herself for the rape, telling herself she should have known better, should have dressed differently, should have come home earlier, and other self-accusations. She was sure that God blamed her.

Molly was also taught that abortion was linked to sexual sin, because it was murder resulting from a woman's sexual choices. Some people from Molly's home church were political activists who picketed abortion clinics and carried signs with images of aborted fetuses. "Women who have abortions will burn in hell," Molly learned at church.

As a result of this teaching, Molly was unable to turn to God during her greatest time of need. Not only did she suffer the pain of rape, the discovery of the resultant pregnancy, and the decision to get an abortion utterly alone, but since then she had carried what at times was unendurable guilt and shame over what had happened to her. Molly's chronic depression and desire to end her life were fueled by images of a wrathful, angry God and threats of hell.

That conversation was the first time Molly learned that nonpunitive understandings of atonement were possible, were biblical, and were within orthodoxy. She could scarcely believe the good news that I shared with her, that God did not want to punish her for what she had endured. The thought that God wanted to heal her grief and bring her into freedom and joy seemed nearly impossible, but she listened eagerly as I assured her that she was truly forgiven for ending her pregnancy. "God has removed your sin as far as the east is from the west," I said, quoting Psalm 103:12. "You told God you were sorry, and God really did hear you and forgive you. Not only that, God saw and continues to see how complicated that situation was. Things are not always as black and white as we think. How much of something like this is sin, and how much is being sinned against? God sees the whole situation, so God is able to forgive us for the part where we are morally responsible and to heal us for all the ways we are hurt. God's love is there bringing wholeness and new-ness of life." For the first time since the rape, Molly began to hope in God's healing love. She began to think that God might be for her and not against her as she tried to heal from her abuse. She had a long way to go in her recovery, but Molly left my office with genuine hope in the healing love of Christ.

The Logic Never Rang True

Many of us survivors have been steeped in the theory of penal substitutionary atonement. We have sung hymns about it in church, have listened to sermons and altar calls based upon this theory, and have been told that we deserve to be crucified for our sins but that Jesus stepped in and took the punishment on our behalf. We were told by preachers to "love" the angry Father God who did this to Jesus and to present ourselves vulnerably to that God in service and worship. Yet the logic never rang true or trustworthy or acceptable to us. Even when we sang the hymns and taught Sunday school and said the penal substitutionary formula about salvation, deep within we were appalled. We knew that with all our human faults we would never subject our children to torture and murder in order to pay off someone's offense. The very idea was unthinkable. Could we be more loving and forgiving than God? Was God a sadist? Was Jesus a masochist? What kind of sick religion was this?

When we allowed ourselves to think deeply about this model, some of us lost our faith. We had to leave the church because we could not stay in a religion that was built on punishment, wrath, and abuse. The God of that religion was exactly like our offenders, and we had to get away. As we headed out the church door, we heard people warning us that we were surely on our way to hell.

Another Way

The strange thing is that the pervasiveness of a penal substitutionary theory of atonement in the church today is by no means supported by the Bible. On the contrary, the New Testament presents several metaphors for atonement, each of them incomplete on its own, each of them helping to address specific questions and contexts.[5] None of these models dominates the others in the Bible. One of the primary biblical metaphors for atonement in the early church was Christus Victor, or Christ who has triumphed over evil and death and who leads his people in victory too. This model is seen in an ancient icon of the resurrection in which Jesus pulls Adam and Eve up out of hell, having triumphed over death on behalf of humankind. The idea that there is only one model of atonement and that it cannot be challenged fails to realize the actual diversity of thought within the Bible and Christian tradition. It contributes to a damaging interpretation of salvation that drives survivors like Molly away from God and the church.

Many liberation theologians reject the doctrine of atonement, and we survivors can understand why. They are like those of us who left the church, unable to come to grips with the notion that any suffering could be redemptive. But we should not surrender what Jesus has actually done in his suffering. He is Emmanuel, God with us, the least of these. Atonement is the healing of the wounds, the forgiveness of the sins, and the making of all things new. It is the reversal of fragmentation, the uncursing of the world. God our Father and Mother, Jesus our Redeemer, and the Holy Spirit our Counselor and Comforter all work together in one accord to bring about the transformation that theologians call atonement.

We should not give up on the doctrine of atonement or the power of what Jesus suffered for us in his passion. What we should surrender is the straightjacket that has bound the theological imagination of the church. Jesus is Emmanuel, God with us. Through every aspect of his life and death, Jesus has chosen solidarity with the least of these. The good news of the gospel is that life, not death, has the final word. Death could not contain Emmanuel. Through the power of his resurrection, we too rise to new life.

For Reflection

For Survivors

1. When I think about Jesus as a victim of sexual abuse:
   a. I feel . . .
   b. I remember . . .
   c. I wonder . . .
   d. I pray . . .
2. Before I read this chapter, my understanding of atonement, if I had one, was that . . .
3. After reading this chapter, I think that atonement means . . .
4. If Molly was in my church . . .

For Those Who Journey with Us

1. When I think about Jesus as a victim of sexual abuse:
   a. I feel . . .
   b. I remember . . .
   c. I wonder . . .
   d. I pray . . .

2. Before I read this chapter, my understanding of atonement, if I had one, was that . . .
3. After reading this chapter, I think that atonement means . . .
4. If Molly was in my church . . .

Recommended Activities

- Watch: *The Green Mile*, *The Chronicles of Narnia: The Lion, the Witch, and the Wardrobe*, *The Lord of the Rings* trilogy
- Create: Assemble a mosaic representing atonement as at-one-ment.

12

In Remembrance of Me

On the night he was betrayed by a companion, Jesus broke bread, gave it to his friends, and told them it was his body. "Do this in remembrance of me," Jesus said, looking around at the faces of people whose feet he had just washed (1 Cor. 11:23b–24). They were about to be plunged into the most shattering grief of their lives. Only later, after the resurrection, did the little band of followers begin to understand what Jesus meant when he lifted the cup and said it was the new covenant in his blood. For the rest of their lives and into countless generations in the future, the table of the Lord would be a table of remembrance.

Every time we celebrate communion, or the Eucharist, we remember Emmanuel, God with us. To remember is to re-member, to bring together into a unified whole that which is broken or scattered. So in the Eucharist we re-member everything about Jesus's life: his healing, his love, his compassion, his courage, his wisdom, his vulnerability, his poverty, his suffering, his death. We remember his resurrection and his promise to come again. *How* we remember Jesus in the

Eucharist can either re-inflict the original wounds of survivors or heal some of our deepest wounds. The Eucharist
is an interpretation of the Bible that we enact physically. It
is a drama that tells some of our most basic beliefs about
salvation, forgiveness, atonement, and grace. It reflects what
we believe or don't believe about God's healing intent for
survivors.

The Controversy

Some theologians today believe that the traditional practice
of the Eucharist is inappropriate, even harmful, for survivors.
This is for two primary reasons. First there is the liturgy,
with patriarchal language and, in many denominations, the
exclusion of women as celebrants. A liturgy that is shaped by
patriarchy perverts the fundamental meaning of the gospel,
which is that in Christ there is neither Jew nor Greek, slave
nor free, male nor female (Gal. 3:28). We are all one in Christ
Jesus. As the old gospel song says, "The ground is level at
the foot of the cross."

Liturgical practices that subordinate women to men by
excluding women as celebrants and by using exclusively male
imagery for God and male language for humanity (references
to humanity in general as "men," "brothers," "sons of God,"
and the like) can sinfully legitimize male supremacy in the
name of God. This practice helps to perpetuate a climate in
which sexual violence against women and children may be
more likely to take place. Survivors have been on the receiving
end of the abuse of power, the majority of which has come
at the hands of men. We know that gender equality in the
theology, language, and practice of liturgy is crucial to the
prevention and healing of sexual abuse. This is doubly true
for those of us whose offenders were male church leaders.

Beyond the problem of patriarchy, there is a second and
deeper problem for some theologians in regard to the Eucha-

rist and survivors: the typical association of the Eucharist with redemptive violence and the theory of penal substitutionary atonement.[1] Only with substantial revision in the theological underpinnings of the Eucharist, they say, can this sacrament be redeemed for survivors.[2] The communion table should be reinterpreted, in other words, using banquet narratives in which Jesus feeds the multitudes or he prepares a meal for his disciples on the beach. All communion narratives using language and images having to do with death, sacrifice, blood, the cross, redemptive suffering, sin, shame, and guilt must be eliminated and replaced with imagery that is nurturing, hopeful, and healing.[3]

On some points I agree with these positions. Reform is in order so that the liturgy and how it is celebrated reflect the egalitarian spirit of Jesus. And we are long overdue for a retrieval of the joy of the Lord's Table. After all, the word *Eucharist* comes from two Greek words meaning "good gift." The word *communion* really does mean "come union," an invitation to intimacy and oneness between Jesus and his people around the table. The very names we use for this expression of worship suggest peace, hope, healing, and welcome.

The practice of the Eucharist ought to be a reflective and healing celebration of Christ's love for us, yet for many people it has become the opposite. In one of the churches I served, I was warned in my first month that attendance would always be lower on communion Sundays. When I asked why, my informer said, "Because it is so depressing." Her perspective is far more widespread than we might think. She and her congregation had been indoctrinated to think of communion as a guilt-laden reflection on the death of Christ, steeped in a penal substitutionary theory of atonement. Once again, one dysfunctional theory of atonement had taken hostage the imagination of the church. As noted in chapter 11, a retrieval of more biblical metaphors for atonement could go a long way to help correct this damaging theology of the Eucharist.

Yet I believe that too much is at stake if we eliminate the biblical narrative in which the Eucharist is traditionally grounded. Jesus was betrayed by a trusted friend, a reality most survivors fully understand because the majority of child sexual abuse happens at the hands of a trusted adult. Jesus's suffering included sexual abuse. Jesus not only loves the least of these, he *was* the least of these. The story of Jesus's suffering, death, and resurrection—his life as one of the least of these—must not be removed or replaced with other, more cheerful stories, especially for us survivors of sexual abuse. On the contrary, when the Eucharist is grounded in the narrative of the least of these, it can become a powerful source of healing for us.

A Long Tradition of Healing

In the earliest days of the church, when the dominant metaphor for atonement was Christus Victor, Christians expected the Eucharist to be a channel for the healing of body, mind, and spirit. The same power that raised Jesus from the dead was available to believers to heal ailments of all kinds, and there was no better way to receive that power than through the Eucharist. For example, a fourth-century liturgical resource for pastors, *Bishop Serapion's Prayer Book*, said, "The sacrament itself was offered as the specific medicine of life unto the healing of every illness."[4] St. Augustine, one of the greatest theologians of all time, expected healings and miracles to accompany the Eucharist. At the time he wrote *The City of God*, his community in Hippo had recorded nearly seventy "attested miracles" in association with the Eucharist.[5]

Expectations of healing continued to shape eucharistic theology for hundreds of years, expressed in the communion hymns of the church (those by St. Thomas Aquinas and Charles Wesley, for example) and in the passionate spirituality of the great Christian saints and mystics. In the Western church, however, particularly among Protestants, the increasing dominance of the penal substitutionary model of atonement overshadowed the therapeutic meanings of the Eucharist so that communion came to be seen overwhelmingly in terms of punishment, law, sin, guilt, blame, and death. The forgetting of the ancient therapeutic theology of the Eucharist has been tragic. The good news, though, is that we do have in the Bible and in ancient Christian tradition the means to heal our theology of the Eucharist. Once again it can become a powerful means of healing in the church, especially for survivors.

Three Ways We Remember

There are at least three ways in which the Eucharist carries unique healing potential for the wounds of sexual abuse, all of them having to do with *how* we remember Jesus at the table. First, as already discussed, we remember that Jesus's suffering, which is represented in the Eucharist, is in solidarity with the suffering of us who have been sexually abused. Thus, in eating the bread and drinking the cup, we "taste" the compassionate love of Jesus, who is with us in our pain. We experience Jesus companioning (a word that literally means "sharing bread with") us as we move from death to resurrection in our own spiritual journeys.

Second, in the Eucharist we remember the risen Christ, whose healing power is mediated as we celebrate his resurrection at the table. We can come to the table of Christus Victor for healing of sexual wounds to body, mind, and spirit. As we taste the bread and cup, we rejoice that sin and evil do not have the last word. Like Adam and Eve in the icon of the resurrection, we feel ourselves being pulled up out of the hell of abuse and its consequences. We are nourished in our new life of healing and liberation.

Third, the Eucharist is a unique, multisensory form of prayer through which we receive the love of Christ physically and intimately. It helps us remember that when Jesus healed people during his earthly ministry he often did so through physical touch. In virtually all of these cases Jesus violated ritual purity codes in touching those who were unclean. For the woman with the issue of blood (Luke 8:43–48), ritual impurity was directly related to her sexuality. Jesus healed the woman's sexual wound with its long years of shame and exclusion, and he did it through physical contact. The Eucharist, of all the ways we can pray, mediates most powerfully the presence of Jesus as a loving, tactile, healing embrace. It is a form of prayer in which we survivors can in some sense "touch Jesus."[6] For survivors, the element of touching and being touched by Jesus carries profound implications.

Holy Women

One of the most pernicious effects of sexual abuse is shame about our bodies and our sexuality. Many of us begin our healing journeys hating our bodies and feeling betrayed by our own sexuality. The goodness of embodied life, a natural enjoyment of our own physicality, has been damaged by the abuse. This is why so many of us struggle with eating disorders and sexual dysfunctions. In the abuse we swallowed shame about our bodies.

In my companionship of survivors of sexual abuse and domestic violence, I have been privileged to hear several stories of divine healing of sexual and bodily shame. Some of these experiences took place as the women received the bread and cup at the communion table. In every case, the women who shared these narratives were tentative, almost afraid to trust their own sacred experience, even though it changed their lives. This was because the experiences came to them unbidden and because they had never heard of such things. Every one of them asked me in her own way, "Am I crazy? Was what I experienced real?" For what the women experienced was the physical, nurturing, noncoercive touch of Jesus. They felt him tenderly loving their bodies by offering himself to them through the Eucharist.

The women shared how the bread and wine were unexpectedly felt as the loving kiss of Christ, or a bodily embrace, or a penetration of divine, healing love, a physical mingling of being between themselves and Christ. For some, communion really was an experience of union with marital overtones. These eucharistic experiences left the women with a deep sense of the sanctity and beauty of their bodies as well as their souls. They experienced an explicit healing of sexual shame because of the Eucharist. Christ came to them gently and offered his body to them in the Eucharist. They were free to receive or to decline. This was an experience of spiritual eros, or desiring love that touched them at the core of their being.

While *eros* is the root word for our word *erotic*, spiritual eros is a beautiful and holy concept that is lost in our degradingly eroticized culture. Throughout Christian history, many of the great saints and mystics have reported experiences of spiritual eros. Often they use the language of romantic love to describe their relationship with Christ. They most often express eros in relationship with the Eucharist.

Hadewijch, the thirteenth-century Flemish Beguine mystic,[7] provides one of the clearest examples of eucharistic experience that manifests as spiritual eros, or the divine union between Christ and his beloved. On Pentecost Sunday, interestingly enough, the day of celebration of the in-filling of the Holy Spirit, Hadewijch writes:

> He gave himself to me in the shape of the Sacrament, in its outward form, as the custom is, and then he gave me to drink from the chalice, in form and taste, as the custom is.
>
> He came himself to me, took me entirely in his arms, and pressed me to him; and all my members felt his in full felicity, in accordance with the desire of my heart and my humanity. So I was outwardly satisfied and fully transported.

. . . Soon, after a short time, I lost that manly beauty outwardly in the sight of his form.

I saw him completely come to naught and so fade and all at once dissolve that I could no longer recognize or perceive him outside me, and I could no longer distinguish him within me. Then it was to me as if we were one without difference.

It was thus: outwardly to see, taste, feel, as one can outwardly taste, see, and feel in the reception of the outward Sacrament. So can the Beloved, with the loved one, each wholly receive the other in all full satisfaction of the sight, the hearing, and the passing away of the one in the other. After that . . . I wholly melted away in him and nothing any longer remained to me of myself.[8]

The eucharistic experience of Hadewijch was an embodied experience of mystical love. Through the Eucharist, she was able to touch the body of Christ, whom she loved, and to experience his love physically touching her. She did not experience the Eucharist in conjunction with a penal substitutionary model of atonement. Instead it was for her a declaration of God's absolute love for her, the sensual embrace of Christ. Jesus was giving his body to her and loving her body in the process. She was drawn into the heart and purposes of God, united with God in a way that integrated her sexuality as a woman. As her experience of bodily union faded, Hadewijch no longer felt separate from God but one with God in God's heart. Afterward she felt herself drawn more closely than ever to God's loving mission in the world.

While not always explicitly named in the context of the Eucharist, the love mysticism found in Mechthild of Magdeburg, St. Teresa of Avila, St. Catherine of Siena, and other Christian mystics interprets union with God as an experience of spiritual eros. The accounts of mystics such as Hadewijch and others share a common theme of divine, healing, energizing, empowering, holy touch. They experience a greater union of themselves with Christ, a healing of gender shame, and an outcome of greater holiness of heart and life. Although mystics such as Hadewijch generally say nothing explicit about being survivors of sexual abuse, their embodied eucharistic experiences of spiritual eros have a direct bearing on the potential for the Eucharist as an agent of healing of sexual shame. They affirm the eucharistic healing stories of some of the women with whom I have journeyed.

The sacramental experiences of spiritual eros described by Hadewijch and other mystics are unknown to average Christians in the pews or to the pastors who shepherd them. In the midst of our abusively eroticized culture, the very idea of spiritual eros is unthinkable to the average Christian. The testimony of mystics like Hadewijch strikes many of my seminary students as at best the bizarre fantasies of sexually repressed women and at worst blasphemy.[9] Just as seminary students struggle to comprehend the meaning of testimonies of women such as Hadewijch, the church continues to labor under burdens of shame, fear, and misinformation when it comes to human sexuality. It is nearly unthinkable for most Christians to link the Eucharist with the healing of sexual shame because of our theological poverty in this area. This is why the women who told me about their experiences were afraid to trust their own experiences of Christ. They had never heard of such things.

In addition to eucharistic experiences of the healing of sexual shame, I have heard testimonies of several women who experienced this kind of healing during visions or dreams with baptismal overtones, not unlike the call vision of nineteenth-century evangelist Julia Foote, who experienced herself being undressed, bathed, and given new clothing by Jesus as part of her call.[10] That is, women described being led into a body of water by Jesus where they were washed, held, baptized, and clothed in new garments. The act of being undressed, bathed, and held was deeply affirming of their bodies and their sexuality. The new clothes represented a removal of shame and a new direction in life. Others have spoken of visions or dreams in which they huddled on the ground in a posture of shame but were lifted to their feet by Jesus, who walked or danced with them joyfully, taking away their shame. In all of these experiences, the women were permanently changed, coming into a much deeper experience of wholeness and release from shame.

Janet Ruffing, a seasoned veteran of Christian spiritual formation, provides extraordinary documentation and analysis of a number of contemporary people who have experienced spiritual eros as part of their maturing spiritual life. Ruffing argues that many spiritual directors do not know how to companion people appropriately in relation to these experiences, much less help survivors find healing through this dimension of spiritual life.[11] Ruffing's work is a critical contribution to the knowledge and skills required for the pastoral care and spiritual guidance of survivors of sexual abuse. The healing of bodily shame and sexual shame are inherent in experiences of love mysticism, a tradition that Ruffing makes accessible for pastoral care.

Tasting Life

In order to help us survivors appropriate the Eucharist as a healing sacrament in relation to the shame of sexual abuse, our spiritual formation needs to include exposure to therapeutic doctrines of atonement, salvation, and sin. We should be helped to see how Jesus's experience of the cross included aspects of sexual abuse so that we know that Jesus knows our pain. We should be taught about the history of healing in the Eucharist. In the context of a recovery group, spiritual direction, or a healing retreat, we should be invited to encounter Hadewijch and other mystics whose experiences of God were affirming of their sexuality. The "love mysticism" of the great Christian mystics, if interpreted well, can be a powerful resource to affirm the goodness of our bodies. In addition to these elements of therapeutic and spiritual care, many good homiletical resources are available that can help pastors preach life-giving messages for us survivors, as well as for the rest of the congregation.[12] When you plan your sermon series, please include these resources in your preparation.

Some of us survivors, especially if we experienced ritual abuse, may never be able to participate in the Eucharist regardless of its interpretation. If this is the case for us, be patient with our struggle. Some of us cannot allow male pastors or priests to put the communion bread into our open mouths because we were orally raped and the body memories are too strong. We may or may not be able to tell you just why we cannot do this. If that is our reality, be kind. Put the wafer or bread into our hands. Let us control what we put into our mouths. Respect our boundaries.

Many of us, given the right support and teaching and companionship, could find significant healing of sexual wounds and shame through the Eucharist. For that to happen, we need pastors, teachers, counselors, and friends who understand the real meaning of the Eucharist. By participating in the sacred meal, we Christians declare our oneness with each other and with the God who made us. We remember the depths of love that bind Jesus to humanity, the love that will not let us go. Through cup and loaf, we see, smell, hold, taste the wonderful gift of Jesus Christ. We taste life, and in the process, we are made whole.

For Reflection

For Survivors

1. In my life I have experienced sexual shame as . . .
2. My experiences of the Eucharist or Holy Communion have been . . .
3. When I think about Jesus giving his body to me in the Eucharist:
   a. I think . . .
   b. I feel . . .
   c. I wonder . . .
   d. I pray . . .

For Those Who Journey with Us

1. My experiences of the Eucharist or Holy Communion have been . . .
2. When I think about Jesus giving his body to me in the Eucharist:
   a. I think . . .
   b. I feel . . .
   c. I wonder . . .

    d. I pray . . .

3. Respond to the concept of divine eros as an experience of some of the great Christian saints and mystics.

Recommended Activities

- Watch: *Babette's Feast, Chocolat*
- Create: Prepare a delicious meal to celebrate the gift of God's healing love in your life. Invite loved ones to share the meal with you.
- Discover: Explore ways that you might get involved in ministries having to do with table fellowship. For example, Meals on Wheels, a food pantry, etc.

13

Letting Go

I replaced the telephone on its cradle, too shocked to speak. "What in the world is the matter?" my husband asked, jumping up from his chair. I struggled to find words. "It's Chuck," I said. "He has been arrested for molesting a child. He is in jail and Barbara is frantic. She is at the police station. I have to go down there." My husband was as stunned as I was. In silence we put our coats on and went out into the snowy night.

Chuck's incarceration was about to become a turning point in my own life, changing me in ways I could not have imagined. I had never provided pastoral care to a sex offender. All of my pastoral ministry in relation to sexual abuse had been for survivors. Up until that night I had thought of sex offenders as animals, or worse. When I preached about God's love for the whole world, when I sang hymns about the forgiveness of God, I did not have offenders in mind. In my heart there was a zone where God's mercy was not welcome, and I simply did not let myself think about the problem with that stance. I wanted offenders to suffer for their deeds. I hoped they would go to hell when they died. I did not want to talk to, work with, or be near them. God had not called me to minister to sex offenders, I believed, only to survivors. Survivors were "us" and offenders were "them."

Then Chuck was arrested.

I could not believe it. Chuck had been a member of our church for years. Surely there was a mistake. It simply could not be true. Chuck was a perpetrator. He was a—the labels rushed through my mind—sex offender, molester, pedophile. Although by then I had experienced deep healing from my own abuse, memories of it rose in a familiar, nauseating wave. How could Chuck do such a thing? What exactly had happened? How could I not have noticed something amiss in him? Surely I should have had some intuition about him. The unanswered questions roared through my mind, leaving me dizzy as I drove to the jail in silence, the windshield wipers dashing back and forth uselessly against the onslaught of snow. Within me a blizzard of conflicting thoughts and feelings raged. One thing was clear: Chuck was in serious trouble. He was going to need me, his pastor. So was Barbara, Chuck's aunt and his closest living relative. She was a white-haired kindergarten teacher with a heart of gold.

As we parked the car and stepped out into the night, my primary feeling was crushing sorrow. Another child now carried the wounds of abuse. Chuck and Barbara's lives would never be the same. I wanted to dehumanize Chuck for his actions, but try as I might I could not do it. There was more to Chuck than this dreadful fact. He was not a monster. He was not a "them"; he was one of "us." Chuck and Barbara were trusted members of the church and good friends to their friends. Whatever Chuck had done, whatever bondage he was in that caused him to sin in this way, he was still a human being. No matter how much revulsion I felt at what he had done, I realized that I still cared about him. I was still his pastor.

When we arrived at the police station, Barbara met us at the door. Her eyes were swollen from weeping. For a few moments no one knew what to say. I simply held her in my arms while she cried. Her stooped shoulders heaved as she kept repeating a question no one could answer. "Why, Chuck? Why?"

My heart broke into a thousand shards of mercy that I did not know I could feel for an offender. I walked down a long corridor to the visitation area, where an officer pointed me toward a cubicle the size of a telephone booth. The jail was nothing new to me. I had visited people there before. A glass window would separate us. Chuck and I would speak to one another through grimy telephones, all of our words recorded and available for the prosecutor's use. How long would Chuck be in jail? When would he be sentenced? Did he have a good lawyer? Would he survive incarceration with hardened criminals? Sex offenders are especially at risk in prison. I had never worried about that before. When I thought about it at all, it seemed to me that they deserved whatever violence came to them behind bars. Another thought flickered through my mind. Had Chuck been molested when he was a child?

Just then the door on the other side of the glass opened and Chuck stepped through, eyes downcast and shoulders slumped. I have never seen anyone more appalled at himself. It was agony to witness his shame. The thought of Chuck's actions against the child brought a fresh wave of revulsion, immediately followed by wrenching grief for Chuck. What was happening to me? Chuck glanced at me, his face panicked. He picked up the phone and held it to his ear, saying nothing. Tears filled his eyes.

I heard words coming out of my mouth as if they were from a stranger.

"Chuck, I want you to know that I am going to be with you through this process, whatever that is going to mean. I don't begin to understand what happened, or why it happened, but I am your pastor and nothing is going to change that. I am here for you. I am still your pastor, maybe now more than ever. God still loves you and I do too." As the words left my mouth, through a sheer gift of grace, suddenly I caught a glimpse of how Christ sees us when we are at our worst. I remembered Julian of Norwich's description of how Christ looks at us in our fallen condition "with pity and not with blame." No one knew better than I that Chuck had committed a grievous sin, an inexcusable wrong. He would have to suffer many hard consequences for his actions. It might be years before he was out of prison. Yet I knew to the depths of my being that Chuck was still redeemable, that not even this abhorrent event could separate him from the love of God.

My heart broke with sorrow for the child he had molested. I knew firsthand how hard it is to heal from sexual abuse. Regardless of how the child was violated, she would now live with the consequences of that sin. Her journey would be permanently marked with this memory and its effects. But what finally undid me was the realization that the same things I felt for the child, I felt for Chuck: pain, dread, sorrow, and compassion. I just sat there and cried.

If You Retain Their Sins

As the months unfolded, I spent much time with Chuck and Barbara. Caring for him required many visits, letters, and telephone calls. It meant advocating for him and learning much more than I already knew about a broken justice system. I also endured contempt from some congregants who learned that I was standing with Chuck as his pastor while he experienced the consequences of his actions. They felt exactly as I once had, that offenders were beyond redemption. Barbara lived those months in a perpetual state of grief. She aged noticeably.

One day after visiting Chuck, I stopped at a coffee shop on the way home. While waiting for the server to take my order, a fragment of a Scripture passage popped into my mind. "If you retain their sins, they are retained." How could I retain someone's sin, I wondered? And why did this come into my mind? Finding a chair in a quiet corner, I reached into my bag for my Bible and journal. The passage was from John 20, a resurrection narrative:

> When it was evening on that day, the first day of the week, and the doors of the house where the disciples had met were locked for fear of the Jews, Jesus came and stood among them and said, "Peace be with you." After he said this, he showed them his hands and his side. Then the disciples rejoiced when they saw the Lord. Jesus said to them again, "Peace be with you. As the Father has sent me, so I send you." When he had said this, he breathed on them and said to them, "Receive the Holy Spirit. If you forgive the sins of any, they are forgiven them; if you retain the sins of any, they are retained." (John 20:19–23)

Somehow there was a link between Jesus "breathing" the Holy Spirit into his disciples and the power to forgive sin. But what did it mean to retain sin? And who but God really had the authority to forgive or retain sin? Why would Jesus say anything about retaining other people's sin when everywhere else he seemed adamant about forgiving it?

Flipping to the small concordance in the back of my Bible, I checked other passages about forgiveness of sin. There was the story of the man who was lowered through the roof (Luke 5:17–26). Apparently his friends' faith was what made his healing and forgiveness possible. Although Jesus said he forgave the man's sin, it is not at all clear that the man asked for forgiveness. I read the conversation of Jesus with Peter, where he said that we must forgive "seventy times seven" the same offense (Matt. 18:21–35). That text came from Jesus's parable of the unmerciful debtor. I remembered, "Forgive us our debts, as we forgive our debtors," a petition that we make every week in church. Turning to Matthew 6, I read the Lord's Prayer and the words that immediately follow it: "For if you forgive others their trespasses, your heavenly Father

153

will also forgive you; but if you do not forgive others, neither will your Father forgive your trespasses" (Matt. 6:12, 14–15). What was God saying to me? On the one hand, I was sure that God said I must forgive others if I wanted God to forgive me. On the other hand, Jesus said that the sins of others that we retain will be retained.

I returned to the original passage that had captured my attention. After he had said "peace be with you," Jesus "breathed on them" and said, "Receive the Holy Spirit." I picked up my steaming mug of coffee and blew gently across the surface, cooling the hot liquid before taking a sip. I thought about the breath of God. How did the breath of Jesus affect the disciples' ability to forgive or retain sins?

I imagined being in the room with the disciples, experiencing the resurrected Jesus. I envisioned Jesus showing us the torture wounds to his hands and the pierced flesh on his torso. These atrocities to the body of God brought back the whole passion narrative with its betrayals and his long, terrible death. One of the last things Jesus said before he died was "Father, forgive them. They do not know what they are doing" (Luke 23:34).

I returned to the image of Jesus breathing on the disciples. When Jesus did this and told them to receive the Spirit, did they think of the creation narratives of Genesis? There too, God breathed divine life into humans. The Spirit of God who hovered like a mother bird over the deeps of Genesis 1 was *Ruach*, meaning Wind, Spirit, and Breath. According to the creation account in Genesis 2, the clay man Adam became a *nephesh*, or living soul, only after the breath of God came into him. What was the connection between becoming a living soul, inhaling the breath of God, and forgiving and retaining sins?

I looked at the passage again. As I read Jesus's apostolic commissioning of those disciples for mission, my eyes were finally opened. "As the Father sent me, so send I you." Jesus's mission from the Father was to love and forgive us with such extraordinary power that we would be released from the captivity of our sin—both the sins we commit and those committed against us. We would have the power to stop our habitual patterns of sin and to forgive those who sinned against us, just as Jesus did. We would have the power to release the toxins from the sins we have endured, from their terrible hold on us. The Holy Spirit, whom Jesus sent, would fill us with so much sacred love, so much holy fire, so much living water that we would be cleansed from the bondage of han. (Recall that han is the concept of the residual aftermath of being sinned against.) Truly, all things could be made new, from the inside out.

But in order for us to experience this renewal, we needed to receive the healing, liberating, renewing Holy Spirit. We would have to breathe in the Holy Spirit, over and over, just as we breathe oxygen to stay alive. This was how we would become "living souls," able to overcome the death-dealing effects of not forgiving. The ability to forgive was part of our re-creation. As I thought of all of this, I remembered how the early church referred to Jesus as Christus Victor, the one who triumphs over sin, death, and hell.

The power to forgive was given to us through the resurrected Christ. Yet we would not automatically forgive others. It would require intentionality in receiving that gift. We could actually choose to "retain" others' sins against us, but it would mean carrying the burden of bitterness and anger, distorting toxins that would prevent us from living the mission of God. Jesus made clear from all his other teachings and his own dying words that forgiveness is at the heart of that mission.

Then I thought of Chuck. How was it that I had reached this place in my life, a time in which I could peacefully and willingly spend precious time and energy with a sex offender, praying for him, listening to his pain, and helping him to come home to the mercy of God? I would never in a hundred years have chosen to do this, nor did I think I was capable of such a thing. There was no question about it. God was the one

155

who brought me into Chuck's crisis, not only to help Chuck but to further heal my soul. Being Chuck's pastor helped me, as nothing else could, to let go of the sins of my offenders.

The Long, Slow Process of Forgiving

One of the worst things the church has done to us survivors in relation to offenders is to lecture us with false doctrines of forgiveness. We have been told in a thousand different ways that if we don't first forgive our offenders of their crimes, God will not forgive us of our sins. We have not been able to comprehend a God who would do this, who would damn a person who was raped as a child if she would not cozy up to her offender when she was an adult. Such a God is an abomination to us.

Too often the message has been that forgiving means allowing the offender back into our lives, especially if he or she is a parent, sibling, or spouse. Often we cannot do that, for our own safety and that of our children. No one who survived and was healed from sexual abuse would make this demand on another.

Forgiving, we have also been told, means forgetting. It means not talking about our pain anymore, or ceasing our efforts to understand how it has shaped us. "Leave the past in the past," well-meaning friends have said. "It's time to forget about what happened and move on." Like Job's friends, ours have not understood the presence of God or the thwarted intent of Satan in our stories. We did not fit into their theological systems.

Such words are knives piercing our hearts. They are duct tape, suffocating us into silence. They are whips, cutting into our souls with threats of hell if we do not forgive and become reconciled to our offenders. Such a message fits with the penal substitutionary theory of atonement, in which God is angry and vengeful, far less merciful or compassionate than flawed humans. Because of the way these ideas are interwoven, many of us shut down the moment we hear a religious person utter the word *forgive*. We dread the impossible demands that will come next.

How we have longed for pastors and teachers who would help us know that forgiveness can be a long, slow process, one that may not be finished this side of glory. We needed to know what forgiveness really is and that all God asks of us is that we be willing to enter the process. Only God can enable this beginning, and only God can bring the journey to completion.

The truth we needed to know is this: the capacity to forgive is a gift from God that finally frees us from the lingering bondage of our abuse. Christus Victor breathes deliverance into us, removing the poisonous residue of sin. Forgiveness is a result of our freedom in Christ, not the payment that we make in order to get it.

To forgive is to keep bringing to God in prayer both the offense and the offender, the sin and its consequences. It is a decision to let God work out full vindication for us and full, final justice for the one who sinned. This doesn't mean that we stop seeking justice for ourselves and others who are wronged. After all, our baptismal vows include resisting evil in all its manifestations and being people who pursue justice and peace. Forgiveness, rather than an abnegation of responsibility to bring justice into the world, means that in our hearts and minds, we willfully entrust ourselves to God's justice and love while we move forward in our lives. On our own we can never achieve full justice or realize the possibility for healing for all who are harmed by sin. So we need the resurrection power of Jesus to come to our aid. Forgiveness is about giving God the "right" to our vindication, God who *wants* to vindicate us and *wants* to make all things new. Unlike our desire for violent retribution, God's justice bears seeds of restoration, making a way for redemption possible for all.

Forgiveness doesn't mean forgetting what happened. How can any of us forget being raped and beaten? To do so would be foolish and could open us to future abuse. Forgiveness means saying no to the poison. It means allowing the Holy Spirit to wash the toxins from the wounds to our souls so that wisdom and compassion spring forth. Forgiveness requires taking stock of what really happened, and it usually begins with feeling our anger and hurt. After a long and truthful time, forgiveness brings us to a new understanding, one that gives us glimpses of how Jesus sees all our sin. As Julian of Norwich saw in her vision of the Servant, Jesus sees beyond our han, beyond our sin, back to the original wounds. His love and healing are applied there. Forgiveness gives us this perspective.

A friend who was abused by her grandfather puts it this way: when we are invited to live our baptism, we are asked to swim in the river of grace. The unwillingness to forgive is like holding on to a branch suspended from the bank, with our bodies already in the water. It requires great effort because we are pulled by the current. We cling to the branch, fearful that if we let go we will drown. God's mercy will be our undoing. But a surprise awaits us when we let go. When we choose not to "retain their sin," when we take the plunge, we find ourselves buoyant in currents of grace that carry us with joy. We become available to participate in God's mercy in this world. To forgive is to let go. Creativity is unleashed, energy flows, new possibilities emerge. Forgiveness is a gift of the Holy Spirit, something that comes as Jesus breathes on us.

Have I retained the sins of my offenders, or have I fully forgiven them? I cannot say for sure because I am still in process. One thing became clear to me that day in the coffee shop. I was able to be Chuck's pastor because a miracle had happened in my heart. I believe forgiveness looks something like that.

For Reflection

For Survivors

1. Chuck's incarceration involved many experiences with the criminal justice system. In what ways has your recovery included contact with police, lawyers, or other official actors within the justice system?
2. Imagine yourself as Chuck's aunt Barbara. What would you have felt and thought upon receiving the terrible news?
3. What are some of the messages you have heard about forgiveness?
4. Imagine Jesus breathing the Holy Spirit upon you and inviting you to receive the power to forgive or retain sins. What do you feel? What do you see?

For Those Who Journey with Us

1. Chuck's incarceration involved many experiences with the criminal justice system. In what ways has your advocacy for survivors included contact with police, lawyers, or other official actors within the justice system?

2. Imagine yourself as Chuck's aunt Barbara. What would you have felt and thought upon receiving the terrible news?

3. Imagine yourself as Chuck's pastor. What would be the most challenging part of providing him with pastoral care?

4. What are some of the theological messages you have heard about forgiveness?

5. Imagine Jesus breathing the Holy Spirit upon you and inviting you to receive the power to forgive or retain sins. What do you feel? What do you see?

Recommended Activities

- Watch: *Dead Man Walking, Crash, The Secret Life of Bees, Schindler's List*

- Create: Use torn pieces of colored paper and glue to create a collage representing the process of forgiveness.

- Discover: Go swimming in a pool where there is a diving board suspended above the water. Take the plunge into the water from the board, reflecting on the process of "letting go of the branch" of bitterness and entering the baptismal water of grace. Be playful in the different ways you dive and jump. Be gentle and kind with yourself emotionally. It is okay not to feel any different in regard to forgiveness afterward, and it is okay to need an indefinite amount of time to forgive. This activity is to help us imagine letting go and trusting God's healing, gracious love in our lives.

- Read: *The Hiding Place* by Corrie ten Boom

14

Final Thoughts

Not long ago while walking in the park, my friend asked, "Will I ever really finish healing from what my father did? I get to a point where I think I'm okay, and it lasts for a few weeks or months, then bam, suddenly something triggers the pain again and I feel almost like I'm starting over. How long is healing going to take? How will I know when I have mostly healed?"

Recovery from sexual abuse is a gradual, spiraling journey, one in which we heal from a memory or a consequence, then circle around, and when our souls are ready, heal again at a deeper level. Our healing brings us freedom and compassion for others. Our scars become catalysts of healing for many others, in ways we see and do not see. Our journey is sacred and it is lifelong.

We survivors bring essential wisdom to biblical interpretation, to theology, and to the practices of pastoral ministry. We believe that our lifelong, often difficult journey to shalom is a great gift to the church, one that should be honored. For our story is told over and over in the Bible. We are Adam and we are Eve. We are the Levite's concubine, Vashti, and Esther. We are eunuchs. We are the woman at the well. We are the Gerasene man. We are the twelve-year-old daughter of Jairus. We are the woman with the issue of blood and Mary weeping at the feet of Jesus. We are bound in love to Jesus, who is in solidarity with us, so we have broken the alabaster jar and poured out for Jesus the graced mystery of our lives.

How long is my friend's healing going to take? How will she know when she has "mostly healed"? Only God knows. But we can be sure of a few realities. Where the Spirit of the Lord is, there is peace. Where the Spirit of the Lord is, there is grace. Where the Spirit of the Lord is, there is love. My sisters and brothers and I, we who were the least of these, want to be where the Spirit of the Lord is. We want others in the church who are weary and heavy laden to join us there, because where the Spirit of the Lord is, we shall all find the healing we seek.

All Things New and the River of Life

We know that the grace we have experienced is not just for survivors of sexual abuse. The cleansing power of Jesus's Word avails for every kind of wound. We survivors who are healing are a sign of the re-creating power of God that is offered to everyone. Through redemption, our stories become Spirit-filled tributaries that flow into God's River of Life. The book of Revelation is an apocalyptic vision that shows us that love will win in the end (Rev. 22:1–7). The vision of John in Revelation lets us know that God our Father and Mother, God the Holy Spirit, and God the Son together have the power, the will, and the love to make all things new. What is most exciting about this book is that it is not just pointing to eternity. The unfolding of the re-creating power of God, in its images and symbols, is a work of grace that God intends for us in our life on earth now. As theologians often put it, the coming of the kingdom of God is both "now" and "not yet." We are invited to live into the promises of Revelation even now, as well as rejoice over the eventual fulfillment of all the promises in the future.

So what does this mean for all of us survivors? The water of life is the Holy Spirit, flowing from the throne of God and the Lamb. That is, the Holy Spirit issues forth from the Creator and the Lamb, with authority to wash and to heal, with the power to re-create our broken lives. The River of Life flows through the Tree of Life, which is the cross of the Lamb. Atonement has brought at-one-ment between us and God, and it is the Holy Spirit who opens our hearts and minds to this gift. The Holy Spirit reveals Christ to us.

As the Spirit/River flows through us, the people of God, it waters the trees on its banks. I believe those trees are "the planting of the Lord" that Isaiah describes in Isaiah 61:1–11. They represent the fulfillment of this promise, in which the redeemed of the Lord have been delivered from all bondage and healed of all their wounds and have become "mighty oaks of righteousness." These "mighty oaks" build up broken people and break the chains of generational sin. Isaiah says they will repair the devastations of many generations. The trees began as "the least of these," tiny acorns. But now they have become a mighty witness to the healing love of God. Where there once was shame there is now a double portion of honor, so the whole cosmos can see the glory of the Lord. The trees represent this profound healing.

In John's vision, the leaves of the trees bring healing to all the nations. This means that all kinds of people will receive the gift of salvation, which heals wounds to body, mind, spirit, and relationships. The fruit from the trees is abundant, something new every month, representing the plentiful nurture that is available to all of us through Christ. Within this verdant paradise, the glory of the Lord will shine like the sun, writes John. This means we see the face of God in Christ, and we are empowered to live entirely for God. The light of Christ shines within us and through us to the rest of creation. No longer do sin, wounds, or han determine our course in life. The very radiance of God illumines our path.

A home with the God who wipes away all tears is the promise of God for every one of us. So is the responsibility to teach, preach, and live into this promise. "Blessed is the one who keeps the words of the prophecy in this book," Jesus says (Rev. 22:7). The promise of healing, the promise of deliverance, and the promise of all things new are not just for someday in heaven. These promises are for God's people today. The River of Life is here, now, today. We keep the words of prophecy when we live as if Jesus speaks the truth.

"Let anyone who wishes take the water of life as a gift," Jesus says, inviting us to receive the Holy Spirit. "I am the Alpha and Omega, the first and the last, the beginning and the end" (Rev. 22:16, 13). Jesus has authority over all that exists. Throughout the world, hundreds of thousands of survivors of sexual abuse are receiving the water of life. We come to the throne of the Lamb. We leave our shame at the cross of Christ, and we know that nothing can separate us from his love. We offer our lives as a witness to the deep love of Christ, from whom our healing flows. We invite you to join us in the shalom that we have found. Come, journey with us.

The Healing Cloud

A Five-Day Retreat Plan for Survivors of Sexual Abuse

The following retreat plan is meant to be carried out over a span of five days, with each day having a theme based on one cloud story in the exodus narrative. It is often the case at retreats that too much information is given—too many talks, books, words, ideas—when what retreatants really need are small, potent portions of artfully presented text from the life-giving Word and ample time, space, and means by which to fully digest them. The whole self—body, mind, and emotions—must have time and space to absorb and be nourished by God through the text.

This retreat is planned for the particular needs and life issues of women who are currently in counseling, survivors who have begun the journey of healing from sexual abuse and are now interested in strengthening their faith and building or exploring for the first time a trusting relationship with God. The retreat probably would not be suitable for a woman who is in the very early stages of recognizing the pervasive effects sexual abuse has had in her life, because of the emotional trauma that is common at an early stage of recovery. The goal of the retreat is to help women see that God is *for* them on their path into freedom and shalom. God is the One who loves them, who has been leading them out of bondage, out of violence, and into an abundant and meaningful life.

The retreat plans are designed to be used in the summer in a retreat center that includes the following facilities: a large, comfortable meeting room; individual accommodations for retreatants; areas for small group discussions; a dining room; a chapel; an art and craft area with supplies; a swimming pool or lake with a swimming beach; several hiking trails in a natural, rural setting; an open field from which large expanses of the sky are visible; and audio-visual equipment, including a DVD player and a CD player. Staff for the retreat should include a director; speaker(s) for sessions; small group discussion leaders; a therapist with specialized training in sexual abuse and domestic violence recovery issues who can be available as needed, or possibly provide input for one or more of the sessions; a spiritual director for optional individual sessions; a massage therapist for retreatants who wish to schedule a massage; a musician to lead singing during worship; clergy (if necessary in keeping with theological traditions) to serve Eucharist at daily chapel services; a lifeguard; and a naturalist for guided hikes.

While this kind of richly resourced retreat is optimal, a much more streamlined plan can work with similarly great effect. It is possible, for example, to hold the retreat in a church or in an urban setting and still find creative ways to provide the learning and prayer experiences that go with each session. What cannot be left out of this kind of healing retreat under any circumstance is adequate professional therapeutic and theological support for retreatants. The safety and spiritually nurturing environment of a healing retreat can sometimes open retreatants to experiences of deep emotional and spiritual distress that can feel overwhelming. These situations require immediate therapeutic attention. Thus, a therapist and a theologically equipped pastor or other Christian leader who is knowledgeable about recovery issues must be part of the retreat staff.

The following plan is primarily an outline, with the messages detailed only in a sparse and suggestive manner, so that the presenters can develop the theme in their own ways.

Daily Schedule

8:00	Morning Prayer	Chapel
8:30	Breakfast	Dining Room
9:30	Morning Session	Conference Room
10:45	Sharing Groups	TBA
12:00	Lunch	Dining Room
1:00–4:30	Massage therapy and individual spiritual direction sessions may be scheduled during these times. Recreation options are also available. Check each day's schedule and suggested response activities for recreation ideas that fit in with the day's theme.	
5:30	Dinner	Dining Room
7:00	Guided Hike	Meeting Place TBA
8:30	Sharing Groups/Stories	TBA
9:30	Evening Prayer with Eucharist	Chapel
10:30	Please observe rule of silence until 8:00 a.m.	

Note: All group and individual activities are optional. If for any reason you wish to omit a scheduled activity, please do so. Please schedule in advance if you wish to have a massage or a private spiritual direction session. Also, unless otherwise scheduled, swimming is restricted to afternoon free hours when the lifeguard is on duty.

167

Day One

- Theme: Led Out of Egypt
- Text: Exodus 13:17–22
- Message

The message should center on the grace of God in leading the people out of Egypt into a new life where they could experience freedom, dignity, and wholeness, and where they would receive the Law (appropriate boundaries that honor God, self, and others). God anticipates the fears and needs of the people and is proactive, leading them by a route that will strengthen them for the long haul. The key word of this text is *lead*, so the key idea of this message is God's leading. The word *lead* in this text may be connected to the shepherding of God in Psalm 23. Other words to highlight include "change their minds" (repent) in verse 17 and "pillar of cloud and fire," verses 21–22. Retreatants should be helped to connect their own flight from bondage to that of the Israelites and to see that God is the One who has led them out in order to give them life. Both during the message and in the small group sessions afterward, retreatants can be helped to identify the "pillar of cloud and fire" in their own journeys and the people who have been "Moses" to them.

Discussion Questions for Small Groups

1. According to verse 17, the Israelites had to go on a winding, longer-than-expected route when leaving Egypt. Tell about the "unexpectedly winding route" in your own "flight from Egypt."
2. According to verse 17, Yahweh knew that if the people faced warfare immediately, they would "repent" of their new freedom and return to bondage because it was familiar. Share about a time you were tempted to "re-

pent" of your new freedom and go back into a chaotic or abusive relationship. What helped you to finally get beyond this temptation?

3. According to verses 21–22, God came to lead the people out of Egypt and into the Promised Land by means of a pillar of cloud and fire. The cloud was a combination of natural elements (the stuff of clouds) and supernatural action (God actually was in the cloud, guiding and protecting them). What are some of the "natural" means God has "divinely infused" to bring you out of bondage and to lead you toward increasing freedom? In other words, what has been your own form of "pillar of cloud and fire"?

4. Who or what has been a "Moses" in your life, guiding, urging, and moving you toward a new life of freedom from shame and oppression?

5. Close your group discussion with prayers of thanksgiving, silent or vocal, for the gift of Moses and the pillar of cloud in our lives.

Suggested Response Activities

1. Follow: In the afternoon, take a guided hike to explore the idea of being led on an unfamiliar trail by a seasoned guide/naturalist.

2. Create: Choose fabric strips or strips of different colors of paper to represent elements of your own process of leaving a relationship of bondage. Weave them into a small mat. If you wish, share your mat with your small group in the evening, telling about the colors and pattern you chose.

3. Converse: In the evening, gather around a communal bonfire. Reflect on the many implications of the pillar of fire and recall the campfires that the Israelites used along their way to the Promised Land.

Day Two

- Theme: A Path through the Sea
- Text: Exodus 14:1–31
- Message

This message should focus on the patience of God with the people's fear, the protection of God during the night as the cloud moved between the Israelites and the Egyptian army, and the power of God in using many elements to achieve a supernatural deliverance. A difficult theological concept that must also be addressed is God's hardening of Pharaoh's heart (14:17). It is vital that the women not see their offenders' cruelty as an act of God literally hardening their offenders' hearts so as to gain eventual glory over the offender. Instead, the women can be helped to see that Pharaoh already had a certain self-chosen hardness of heart toward God and the Israelites, and in a sense, God was allowing this hardness to reach its logical conclusion. (There is a genuine parallel in the lives of many women who are survivors of domestic violence, in their former partners' "battering cycles" seeming to soften, then becoming harder and more violent with each episode.) This message should also include reflections on God's ordering of primordial creation elements (earth, water, wind, and fire, with allusions to the primordial chaos of Gen. 1) in the deliverance of God's people and its parallel in the retreatants' lives, as they have seen God bringing order out of chaos in their own lives.

Discussion Questions for Small Group

1. In verses 10–14, the Israelites became panic-stricken as they realized the Egyptians were in hot pursuit. This was their first real challenge to live the new way of freedom and trust in God instead of the old way of oppression. In their fear they "remembered" Egyptian

bondage as being not so bad after all. They blamed Moses for talking them into leaving Egypt and were sure that they were about to die. What they needed was a reality check as to the way life actually had been for them in bondage. How did God help them during their weakness and fear in this episode? How is their selective memory about Egypt similar to the selective memory of survivors who as adults are trying to decide whether to leave chaotic and abusive relationships?

2. In verses 19–20, the pillar of cloud and fire moved around behind the Israelites, protecting them and hiding them from their pursuers. Share about your own experience of being "hidden, protected, and provided for" as you moved through the initial crisis of choosing to heal from sexual abuse.

3. God used the primordial elements of creation (earth, water, wind, and fire) to bring about the deliverance of the Israelites. In this way the story is reminiscent of the creation account in Genesis 1. Where do you most feel a need for God to bring new order into your life?

4. What does this passage say to you about God's character? About God's view of shame and oppression? About God's attitude toward us when we are weak and fearful?

Suggested Response Activities

1. Watch: In the afternoon, ask a friend to join you for a movie about women coming into freedom and wholeness. Talk about which character you most identify with. Choose from *Fried Green Tomatoes*, *How to Make an American Quilt*, *The Color Purple*, or *The Joy Luck Club*.

2. Create: Make a mixed-media collage using seeds, small stones, string, twigs, and other natural objects as a

reflection on God bringing order out of chaos in order to create new life for God's people. If you wish, share the collage with your small group in the evening.

3. Enjoy: Weather permitting, watch the sunset from a good vantage point outdoors. Notice the many fragrances, sounds, and sights of nature as you are present to the sunset. Reflect on God's presence revealed in the fiery colors of the sunset and the other sensory experiences of nature. If you wish, journal about the feelings that surface as you watch the sunset.

Day Three

- Theme: Celebrating Our Victories
- Text: Exodus 15:1–21
- Message

Begin with the fact that Miriam's song was the original version of this victory song (helping retreatants see that Miriam was a strong woman and one who had standing in her faith community). Discuss the importance of naming in this song (vv. 1–12): the naming of the Lord as Victor and Champion, the naming of the enemy, the naming of the victory, the naming of deliverance. Help retreatants link this to their experience in therapy of naming their pain, their need, the injustice, and their feelings concerning coming into freedom. (Such naming is essential to recovery and to beginning a process of forgiveness of the offender.) Hope for the future in verses 13–18 is based on the powerful victory of the recent past. Encourage retreatants to reimagine the future as a hopeful, God-directed adventure based on the powerful experience of deliverance they have had in the recent past. Notice the dance of joy led by the Israelite women in this passage. The whole body (the *female* body) is used in worship and praise, and God is pleased with their offering of dance. (For abuse survivors, there are often problems with body image and shame. This text helps to affirm both embodiment and sexuality as sacred gifts.)

Discussion Questions for Small Groups

1. Take fifteen minutes and write your own version of your victory song, naming events and persons and celebrating your own "crossing of the sea." Imagine it being sung by a mighty chorus of women with strong, clear voices. Read your victory songs to one another. (As always, sharing is on a volunteer basis.)
2. As you look to the future in light of your own crossing of the sea, what are some of your hopes and dreams?
3. How does it feel when you imagine Miriam, a woman, and her group of singers leading all of Israel in the victory song and dance?
4. Imagine yourself leading a victory dance concerning your own liberation. Describe your victory dance garments. What would be the ideal setting for the dance? Would the dance be slow and meditative or fast and energetic? Who would you invite to watch and listen?

Suggested Response Activities

1. Journey: In the afternoon, go to the pool to swim. Walk through the water in the shallow end, reflecting on the "path through the sea" for the Israelites and "the path through the sea" in your own life. Then float or gently bob in deeper water, reflecting on the love and grace of God that has carried you thus far. Feel the water gracefully supporting the weight of your body. Experience God's love for your body and your womanhood as the water holds you.
2. Create: Use pastels, finger paint, or crayon on large paper to create an image that evokes the crossing of

the "Red Sea" in your own journey. If you wish, share the creation with your small group in the evening.

3. Move: In the evening, join the other women around the bonfire or in the conference room for a joyful time of music and simple folk/liturgical dance, using rhythm instruments. Celebrate your own crossing of the sea!

Day Four

- Theme: My Presence Will Go with You
- Text: Exodus 33:12–23
- Message

A key idea in this passage is the importance of God knowing and calling Moses "by name." God's presence is not just transcendent in the cloud and fire but very personal and intimate: God knows us by name. Both "know" and "name" are richly nuanced with the ideas of intimacy and union. The message should help the women explore what it means that God knows them intimately, by name, and that God wishes to go with them, give them rest (v. 14), and show favor to them. God also wishes to continue to reveal God's self to the women, just as God did for Moses. The theme of intimate prayer as listening and watching for "God's glory" (vv. 17–23), and as speaking with God as with a friend, should be highlighted. Such prayer is indispensable in the journey to wholeness with God. Moses hungered to "see God," which was pleasing to God. Even though Moses could not experience absolute, unbroken union with God, God was willing to give Moses as much revelation and union as Moses could receive. The idea that God loves to give God's self to us and wants to be intimate with us is very healing for women who have suffered abuse. It helps them to see that they are lovable, desirable, strong, and worthy of intimacy.

Discussion Questions for Small Groups

1. Why do you think it was important for Moses to know that God knew him and called him "by name"?
2. What kinds of images and feelings surface when you think of God knowing you and calling you "by name"?
3. If God were to give you a loving and affirming nickname, what do you think it might be?
4. What are some ways we can deepen our ability to pray "listening and watching for God" prayers?
5. How have you "seen God passing by" most recently in your journey?

Suggested Response Activities

1. Discover: In the afternoon, take a hike through the woods and look for clefts in rocks or in tree trunks, where small animals make their homes, plants are growing. Think about the refuge the cleft is for these living things, and the strong refuge God's love is for us.
2. Write: Journal a dialogue between yourself and God, based on the theme of God's name for you and God's desire for an intimate relationship with you.
3. Create: Use clay to sculpt a form that represents your own experience of being safely hidden in the "cleft of the rock," from which you came to see and understand God in a deeper way.
4. Tell: Before evening prayer, have a time of bedtime stories, with popcorn, hot cocoa, and the following children's picture books, which reinforce the idea of God's self-revealing, steadfast, *hesed* love for us: *The Runaway Bunny* by Margaret Wise Brown, *Mama, Do You Love Me?* by Barbara M. Joosse, *Guess How Much I Love You* by Sam McBratney, *Where the Wild Things Are* by Maurice Sendak.

Day Five

- Theme: Keeping on the Path
- Text: Exodus 34:1–16; 40:34–38
- Message

This message is in many ways a capstone for the week's journey, designed to send the women away with hope, courage, and commitment to their ongoing journey with God. It should highlight the following four themes from the text: the effects of generational sin and God's power to break the cycle (34:5–7); the hard work of recovery takes time and requires commitment to keep going even though we stumble along the way (vv. 8–9); a commitment to recognize destructive relationships, thought patterns, and idols in our lives and to get rid of them instead of trying to make treaties with them (vv. 10–16); and the necessary centrality of God's presence (the cloud) and leading in our lives in order for us to be whole and free (34:10; 40:34–38). All these are necessary in order to fully heal. All of them involve individual commitments that are lived out in the context of community.

Discussion Questions for Small Groups

1. In verses 11–16, God warns the Israelites not to "make covenants" of any kind with people who will emotionally and spiritually ensnare them and lead them into yet another kind of bondage. He warns them not to worship any other gods because only God is God. Based on the message and what you may have already known about these Canaanite cultures, why were they so tempting to the Israelites? What were the emotional and spiritual "hooks"?

2. Think about your own journey. What are the emotional and spiritual "hooks" of your potentially destructive relationships and your potential idols? What can we do when we feel ourselves leaning toward a "hook"?

3. As we have seen, God's love is powerful enough to break the cycle of generational sin and to help people start a new life free from the cycle of abuse. What are two or three ways in which you intend to hand "wholeness" on to your children or grandchildren? (If you don't have children or grandchildren, what are two or three ways other women could do this, or that you could help cultivate freedom from abuse in the next generation in your church or community?)

Suggested Response Activities

1. Pray: In the afternoon, swim laps or take a leisurely walk for twenty minutes, using your swim strokes or the stride of your walk as a kind of metronome to repeat the short prayer: "Merciful and gracious, God abounds in love" (based on Exod. 34:6–7).
2. Create: Assemble a string of prayer beads with which to pray Psalm 103, which is related to the Exodus text for today's session. Choose twenty-two beads, one for each verse, and choose each bead's color and size to express the meaning of its verse. If you wish, share your beads with your group in the evening.
3. Remember: In the evening, gather around a bonfire for a time of thanksgiving for the week, to bring the week to closure. Begin with singing some of the songs that have been used in the prayer services during the week, such as "Be Not Afraid." Each woman should have written on a piece of paper three gifts she has received from the week. Each woman takes a turn reading her thanksgiving list, then as she casts it into the fire to help create the "smoke of prayer" that "ascends to God," all the women sing a brief chorus of thanksgiving, prepared by the worship leader. At the conclusion, everyone joins hands and sings a suitable "song of sending."

A Definition of Sexual Abuse

The following definition of sexual violence is taken from the Faith Trust Institute website:

> Sexual violence refers to harmful behaviors that use sex or sexuality as a weapon to control, intimidate or violate others. Whether it is viewed clinically or legally, objectively or subjectively, violence is the common denominator. Sexual violence is about violence that misuses sex and sexuality to exert power over or exploit others. It encompasses rape, incest, assault, date rape, sexual exploitation, misconduct and abuse, as well as inappropriate touching and harassing jokes and comments. The injuries may be psychological or physical, and frequently are both.[1]

Sexual violence occurs in public and private places: in homes, workplaces, schools, and religious communities. Yet sexual violence is not often discussed in religious settings. The silence contributes to misunderstandings and myths that

179

blame the victims. A lack of understanding can also lead to the misuse of sacred texts to justify sexually abusive behavior.

There are many ways communities of faith can help prevent sexual violence, including learning about the underlying causes of sexual violence as a social problem. We can work toward building a community free of sexual violence that seeks the safety and well-being of all.

Recommended Resources

Articles and Papers

Heath, Elaine A. "Altar Tears." *Journal of Religion and Abuse* (Winter 2006): 5–6.

———. "Jabez, a Man Called Pain." *Ashland Theological Journal* 33 (2001): 7–16.

———. "The Levite's Concubine: Domestic Violence and the People of God." *Priscilla Papers* 13, no. 1 (Winter 1999): 10–20.

Liston, Pamela Harrell. "Sex Trafficking: Overview Analysis and the Church's Response." Unpublished paper presented to Perkins School of Theology, Dallas, TX, May 2, 2008.

Books

Allender, Dan B. *The Wounded Heart: Hope for Adult Victims of Childhood Sexual Abuse.* Colorado Springs: NavPress, 1990.

Augustine. *The City of God.* Translated by Henry Bettenson. New York: Penguin, 1984.

Baker, Mark D., ed. *Proclaiming the Scandal of the Cross: Contemporary Images of Atonement.* Grand Rapids: Baker Academic, 2006.

Brueggemann, Walter. "The Book of Exodus: Introduction, Commentary, and Reflections." In *The New Interpreter's Bible*, vol. 1, 675–981. Nashville: Abingdon, 1994.

———. *Genesis.* Atlanta: John Knox Press, 1982.

Carnes, Patrick. *Don't Call It Love: Recovery from Sexual Addiction.* New York: Bantam, 1992.

Diamant, Anita. *The Red Tent*. New York: Picador, 1997.

Farley, Wendy. *The Wounding and Healing of Desire: Weaving Heaven and Earth*. Louisville: Westminster John Knox, 2005.

Ferree, Marnie C. *No Stones: Women Redeemed from Sexual Shame*. Fairfax, VA: Xulon Press, 2002.

Flake, M. Elaine McCollins. *God in Her Midst: Preaching Healing for Wounded Women*. Valley Forge, PA: Judson Press, 2007.

Foote, Julia. "A Brand Plucked from the Fire: An Autobiographical Sketch." In *Sisters in the Spirit: Three Black Women's Autobiographies of the Nineteenth Century*, edited and with an introduction by William Andrews, 161–234. Bloomington, IN: Indiana University Press, 1986.

Fortune, Marie M. "Toward a Feminist Theology of Religion and the State." In *Violence against Women and Children: A Christian Theological Sourcebook*, edited by Marie M. Fortune and Carol J. Adams, 15–35. New York: Continuum, 1995.

Fortune, Marie M., and Carol J. Adams, eds. *Violence against Women and Children: A Christian Theological Sourcebook*. New York: Continuum, 1995.

Goudy, June Christine. *The Feast of Our Lives: Re-imaging Communion*. Cleveland: Pilgrim Press, 2002.

Green, Joel B., and Mark D. Baker. *Recovering the Scandal of the Cross: Atonement in New Testament and Contemporary Contexts*. Downers Grove, IL: InterVarsity Press, 2000.

Hadewijch. *Hadewijch: The Complete Works*. Edited by Columba Hart. Classics of Western Spirituality. New York: Paulist Press, 1980.

Hall, Thelma. *Too Deep for Words: Rediscovering Lectio Divina*. New York: Paulist Press, 1988.

Haugen, Gary A. *Good News about Injustice*. Downers Grove, IL: InterVarsity Press, 1999.

Heath, Elaine A. *The Mystic Way of Evangelism: A Contemplative Vision for Christian Outreach*. Grand Rapids: Baker Academic, 2008.

Julian of Norwich. *Showings*. Classics of Western Spirituality, edited by Edmund Colledge and James Walsh. New York: Paulist Press, 1978.

Kasl, Charlotte S. *Women, Sex, and Addiction: A Search for Love and Power*. New York: HarperOne, 1990.

Kelsey, Morton. *Psychology, Medicine, and Christian Healing*. New York: HarperSanFrancisco, 1988.

Kiuchi, Nobuyoshi. *Leviticus*. Apollos Old Testament Commentary Series. Downers Grove, IL: IVP Academic, 2007.

Lamott, Anne. *Traveling Mercies: Some Thoughts on Faith*. New York: Pantheon Books, 1999.

Linn, Dennis, Sheila Fabricant Linn, and Matthew Linn. *Sleeping with Bread: Holding What Gives You Life*. New York: Paulist Press, 1995.

Milhaven, Annie Lally, ed. *Sermons Seldom Heard: Women Proclaim Their Lives*. New York: Crossroads, 1991.

Motyer, J. A. "Curse." In *New Bible Dictionary*. 2nd ed. CD-ROM. Wheaton: Tyndale, 1982; Oak Harbor, WA: Logos Research Systems, 1997.

Murk-Jansen, Saskia. *Brides in the Desert: The Spirituality of the Beguines*. Maryknoll, NY: Orbis, 1998.

Niditch, Susan. "Genesis." In *The Women's Bible Commentary*, edited by Carol A. Newsom and Sharon H. Ringe, 13–29. Louisville: Westminster John Knox, 1998.

Park, Andrew Sung. *The Wounded Heart of God*. Nashville: Abingdon, 1993.

Park, Andrew Sung, and Susan L. Nelson, eds. *The Other Side of Sin*. Albany, NY: The State University of New York Press, 2001.

Pipher, Mary. *Reviving Ophelia*. New York: Ballantine Books, 1994.

Procter-Smith, Marjorie. *Praying with Our Eyes Open*. Nashville: Abingdon, 1995.

———. "The Whole Loaf: Holy Communion and Survival." In *Violence against Women and Children: A Christian Theological Sourcebook*, edited by Marie M. Fortune and Carol J. Adams, 464–78. New York: Continuum, 1995.

Ruffing, Janet. *Spiritual Direction: Beyond the Beginnings*. New York: Paulist Press, 2000.

Scruton, Roger. *Sexual Desire: A Moral Philosophy of the Erotic*. New York: Continuum, 1986.

Simons, Walter. *Cities of Ladies: Beguine Communities in the Medieval Low Countries, 1200–1565*. Philadelphia: University of Pennsylvania Press, 2001.

Spencer, F. Scott. "Eunuch." In *The New Interpreter's Dictionary of the Bible: D–H*, 355–56. Vol. 2. Nashville: Abingdon, 2007.

ten Boom, Corrie. *The Hiding Place*. New York: Bantam, 1984.

Trible, Phyllis. *Texts of Terror: Literary-Feminist Readings of Biblical Narratives*. Philadelphia: Fortress Press, 1984.

Van Selms, A. "Balaam." In *New Bible Dictionary*. 2nd ed. CD-ROM. Wheaton: Tyndale, 1982; Oak Harbor, WA: Logos Research Systems, 1997.

Walls, Jeannette. *The Glass Castle*. New York: Scribner, 2005.

Wenham, Gordon J. *Leviticus*. New International Commentary on the Old Testament. Grand Rapids: Eerdmans, 1994.

Westermann, Claus. *Genesis 1–11*. Minneapolis: Augsburg, 1984.

Wilkinson, Bruce. *The Prayer of Jabez*. Sisters, OR: Multnomah Press, 2000.

Young, William P. *The Shack*. Newbury Park, CA: Windblown Media, 2007.

Children's Books

Brown, Margaret Wise. *The Runaway Bunny*. New York: HarperCollins, 2005.

Eastman, P. D. *Are You My Mother?* New York: Random House, 1960.

Joosse, Barbara M. *Mama, Do You Love Me?* Vancouver, BC: Raincoast Books, 1991.

McBratney, Sam. *Guess How Much I Love You.* Somerville, MA: Candlewick Press, 2008.

Sendak, Maurice. *Where the Wild Things Are.* New York: HarperCollins, 1988.

Movies

Babette's Feast, directed by Gabriel Axel (1987; Denmark: MGM, 2001), DVD.

Billy Elliot, directed by Stephen Daldry (United Kingdom: Universal Focus, 2001), DVD.

Chocolat, directed by Lasse Hallström (France: Miramax, 2001), DVD.

The Color Purple, directed by Steven Spielberg (1985; United States: Warner Bros, 2003), DVD.

Crash, directed by Paul Haggis (United States: Lionsgate, 2005), DVD.

The Chronicles of Narnia: The Lion, the Witch, and the Wardrobe, directed by Andrew Adamson (United States: Walt Disney Pictures, 2006), DVD.

Dead Man Walking, directed by Tim Robbins (United States: MGM, 2000), DVD.

Diary of a Mad Black Woman, directed by Tyler Perry. (United States: Lionsgate, 2005), DVD.

Enough, directed by Michael Apted (United States: Columbia Pictures, 2002), DVD.

Forrest Gump, directed by Robert Zemeckis (1994; United States: Paramount Pictures, 2001), DVD.

Fried Green Tomatoes, directed by Jon Avnet (1991; United States: Universal Pictures, 1998), DVD.

Girl, Interrupted, directed by James Mangold (United States: Columbia Pictures, 2000), DVD.

The Green Mile, directed by Frank Darabont (United States: Warner Bros., 2000), DVD.

How to Make an American Quilt, directed by Jocelyn Moorhouse (1995; United States: Universal Pictures, 1999), DVD.

The Joy Luck Club, directed by Oliver Stone (1993; United States: Hollywood Pictures, 2002). DVD.

Juno, directed by Jason Reitman (Canada: Fox Searchlight, 2008), DVD.

Little Miss Sunshine, directed by Jonathan Dayton and Valerie Faris (United States: Fox Searchlight Pictures, 2006), DVD.

The Lord of the Rings trilogy, directed by Peter Jackson (New Zealand: New Line Cinema, 2002–04), DVD.

Reign Over Me, directed by Mike Binder (United States. Columbia Pictures, 2007), DVD.

Roots, directed by Marvin J. Chomsky, John Erman, David Greene, and Gilbert Moses (1977; United States: Warner Home Video, 2007), DVD.

Schindler's List, directed by Steven Spielberg (United States: Universal Pictures, 2004), DVD.

The Secret Life of Bees, directed by Gina Prince-Bythewood (United States: Fox Searchlight, 2009), DVD.

Slumdog Millionaire, directed by Danny Boyle and Loveleen Tandan (United States: Twentieth Century Fox, 2009), DVD.

Whale Rider, directed by Niki Caro (New Zealand: Newmarket Films, 2003), DVD.Stone, Oliver. *The Joy Luck Club*. DVD. United States: Hollywood Pictures, 2002.

Zemeckis, Robert. *Forrest Gump*. DVD. United States: Paramount Pictures, 2001.

Websites

American Institute on Domestic Violence. www.aidv-usa.com.

Epiphany Academy of Formative Spirituality. www.epiphanyassociation.org.

Faith Trust Institute. www.faithtrustinstitute.org.

Genesis Women's Shelter. www.genesisshelter.org.

National Center for Victims of Crime. www.ncvc.org.

National Coalition Against Domestic Violence. www.ncadv.org.

Rape Victim Advocacy Program. www.rvap.org.

U.S. Department of Health and Human Services. www.acf.hhs.gov.

Notes

Chapter 1

1. The national statistics for abuse for both genders are staggering. While both men and women are victims of sexual abuse and domestic violence, 95 percent of domestic violence is against women. Twice as many girls as boys are victimized by sexual abuse, with one out of three girls and one out of six boys experiencing sexual abuse before the age of eighteen. Faith Trust Institute, "Q&A," www.faithtrustinstitute.org/; Rape Victim Advocacy Program, "Myths and Facts—Child Sexual Abuse," www.rvap .org/pages/myths_and_facts_about_child_sexual_abuse; American Institute on Domestic Violence, "Domestic Violence in the Workplace Statistics," www .aidv-usa.com/Statistics.htm; and National Coalition Against Domestic Violence, "Domestic Violence Facts," www.ncadv.org/files/DomesticViolenceFact Sheet(National).pdf.

2. My definition of evangelism is the process of holistic initiation of persons into a holy life, revealed in Jesus Christ, empowered by the Holy Spirit, surrendered to the reign of God for the transformation of the world. Holiness is about giving ourselves completely to God and being in partnership with God in this world. It is a dynamic, daily process of receiving and giving the love of God. There are many people in the church who, like Laura, attend church and are members of the church but have never been evangelized.

3. At that time I used the New International Version or the King James Version of the Bible.

Chapter 2

1. Hermeneutic is a method or set of principles for interpretation.

2. Andrew Sung Park prefers the doctrine of original "han" instead of original sin. He draws from the Korean concept of han, which is the accumulation of bitterness, shame, anger, despair, and other destructive attitudes and feelings that result from experiences of being sinned against. Park's work is enlightening to this discussion of sexual abuse but especially focuses on

186

han brought about by the systemic oppression of racism, classism, and sexism. Andrew Sung Park, *The Wounded Heart of God* (Nashville: Abingdon, 1993); and Andrew Sung Park and Susan L. Nelson, eds., *The Other Side of Sin* (Albany, NY: The State University of New York Press, 2001).

3. My reading of this text has also been inspired by Phyllis Trible's hermeneutic of the Bible that honors the victims of violence in the Bible who are so often nameless and voiceless women. Phyllis Trible, *Texts of Terror: Literary-Feminist Readings of Biblical Narratives* (Philadelphia: Fortress Press, 1984).

4. Saint Irenaeus's exact dates of birth and death are not clear, but he lived in the second century, was Bishop of Lyons, and died around the beginning of the early third century.

5. Julian (ca. 1342–1417) experienced a series of sixteen christological visions that in light of Scripture and Christian tradition became her primary source of theological reflection for the rest of her life. Within the visions Julian saw fallen humanity as one person, "the servant." In Pauline terms, she saw first and second Adam as one servant, simultaneously corporate humanity (Adam) and Christ. In her vision, Christ is bound to humanity forever in infinite love. The servant parable (chap. 51) is pivotal to understanding the rest of her visions and her theology. Julian of Norwich, *Showings*, ed. and with an introduction by Edmund Colledge and James Walsh, Classics of Western Spirituality (New York: Paulist Press, 1978).

6. Claus Westermann, *Genesis 1–11* (Minneapolis: Augsburg, 1984), 186; and Susan Niditch, "Genesis," in *The Women's Bible Commentary*, ed. Carol A. Newsom and Sharon H. Ringe (Louisville: Westminster John Knox, 1998), 16. Indeed, as ancient exegetical approaches demonstrate, a text can have numerous meanings at the same time. This is part of the reason that the Bible is "living and active."

7. My interpretation of Genesis 3 appears in a shorter and somewhat different form, focusing on hamartiology and the doctrine of atonement, in my book *The Mystic Way of Evangelism: A Contemplative Vision for Christian Outreach* (Grand Rapids: Baker Academic, 2008).

8. The Hebrew concept of "knowing" is holistic, nuanced with participation in that which is known, unlike the Enlightenment concept of knowledge as supposedly objective intellectual awareness of that which is known.

9. As Walter Brueggemann notes, this text is more concerned "with faithful responses and effective coping" in a world in which evil exists than in the origins of evil. The mystery of iniquity is unexplained. Walter Brueggemann, *Genesis* (Atlanta: John Knox Press, 1982), 41.

10. Westermann insightfully comments, regarding the nature of the temptation, that "at bottom what entices a person to transgress a limit is not the sensual pleasure heightened even more by the prohibition, but the new possibilities of life that are apparently opened by the transgression." Westermann, *Genesis*, 249.

11. Rape Victim Advocacy Program, "Myths and Facts—Child Sexual Abuse," www.rvap.org/pages/myths_and_facts_about_child_sexual_abuse.

12. When Adam first meets Eve in Genesis 2:23, he calls her "bone of my bone, flesh of my flesh" and names her *Isha*, the Hebrew word that sounds like

Ish, the word for man, underscoring their equality. While "Eve" is a positive name, "mother of all the living," the former equality of the man and woman has been broken.

13. Many of these strategies are described in Dan B. Allender, *The Wounded Heart: Hope for Adult Victims of Childhood Sexual Abuse* (Colorado Springs: NavPress, 1990). Andrew Sung Park describes the residual effects of "disgrace shame" that is left in victims of oppression, including sexual abuse victims, as disgust with the self, feelings of deficiency, abandonment, defectiveness, and defilement. Park, *The Wounded Heart of God*, 83–84. For a related discussion of the pervasive effects of shame from child sexual abuse from the perspective of moral philosophy, see Roger Scruton, *Sexual Desire: A Moral Philosophy of the Erotic* (New York: Continuum, 1986), 295–98, 311–15.

14. Faith Trust Institute, "Q&A," www.faithtrustinstitute.org/. Many survivors do not understand how the abuse has affected them until well into adult life, if ever. Most survivors of child sexual abuse do not become sexual abusers as adults. The wounds of sexual abuse do result in many kinds of attitudes and behaviors that then become the source for additional wounding and sin, which may or may not be sexual. For example, a survivor may become enslaved to sin against herself in allowing herself to live in a relationship of domestic abuse as an adult. In all of this it is important to keep in mind that victims of child sexual abuse are not responsible for their abuse, and victims of domestic violence of any kind neither deserve nor cause the violence of their offenders. See Rape Victim Advocacy Program, "Myths and Facts—Child Sexual Abuse," www.rvap .org/pages/myths_and_facts_about_child_sexual_abuse; and the National Center for Victims of Crime, "Child Sexual Abuse," www.ncvc.org/ncvc/main. aspx?dbName=DocumentViewer&DocumentID=32315. For more about the sins of sexual abuse and domestic violence from a Christian perspective, see Marie M. Fortune and Carol J. Adams, eds., *Violence against Women and Children: A Christian Theological Sourcebook* (New York: Continuum, 1995). Also see Allender, *The Wounded Heart*.

15. Chapter 7, "Are You My Mother?" addresses the mother wounds of survivors.

Chapter 3

1. Emilie Townes is a leading womanist theologian whose thought reflects the perspectives and voice of African American women. Other well-known womanists are Karen Baker-Fletcher and Renita Weems. James Cone and Cornell West are prominent black liberation theologians.

2. "Go Down Moses," Afro-American spiritual, adapted and arranged by William Farley Smith, 1986, *The United Methodist Hymnal* (Nashville: The United Methodist Publishing House, 1989), 448–49.

3. Ibid.

4. Walter Brueggemann, "The Book of Exodus: Introduction, Commentary, and Reflections," in *The New Interpreter's Bible*, vol. 1 (Nashville: Abingdon, 1994), 788.

5. The explicit identification of God the Creator in the Exodus theophany is found in one of the deuterocanonical texts of the Bible, Wisdom 19:6.

6. This perspective on the power of Christ is called a "high Christology" in systematic theology.

Chapter 4

1. Genesis offers a wide array of services to help battered people heal, including counseling, advocacy, and programs to educate religious communities, schools, and the police about the problem of domestic violence. See www.genesisshelter.org/index.php.

2. This chapter draws from my article "The Levite's Concubine: Domestic Violence and the People of God," *Priscilla Papers* 13, no. 1 (Winter 1999): 10–20. *Priscilla Papers* is a journal of Christians for Biblical Equality, an evangelical feminist organization that provides resources and support for egalitarian leadership in church, home, and society. See www.cbeinternational.org.

3. For this narrative I am indebted to the work of Phyllis Trible. See Trible, *Texts of Terror: Literary-Feminist Readings of Biblical Narratives* (Philadelphia: Fortress Press, 1984).

4. Ibid., 66.

5. The Masoretic text is the complete Hebrew Bible that was translated between the seventh and tenth centuries AD.

6. The Syriac texts of the Bible are very old, dating back to the early centuries of the church.

7. The Septuagint (the LXX) is an ancient Greek translation of the Hebrew Bible, translated during the intertestamental period, between the third and first centuries BC.

8. The Old Latin texts date back to the third century AD.

9. Trible, *Texts of Terror*, 66.

10. Ibid., 80.

Chapter 5

1. Pamela Harrell Liston, "Sex Trafficking: Overview Analysis and the Church's Response," an unpublished paper presented at Perkins School of Theology, Dallas, TX, May 2, 2008, 3.

2. Ibid.

3. U.S. Department of Health and Human Services, "Sex Trafficking Fact Sheet," www.acf.hhs.gov/trafficking/about/fact_sex.pdf.

4. "The Murder of Emmett Till," *American Experience*, www.pbs.org/wgbh/amex/till.

5. Ibid.

Chapter 6

1. Matthew, Dennis, and Sheila Fabricant Linn are internationally beloved writers and retreat leaders whose gifts are especially helpful for people recovering from trauma. I have used their delightfully illustrated "adult theology picture books" (my term, not theirs) as resources in pastoral care, retreats, and spiritual direction with survivors. See Dennis Linn, Sheila Fabricant Linn,

and Matthew Linn, *Sleeping with Bread: Holding What Gives You Life* (New York: Paulist Press, 1995).

2. Elaine A. Heath, "Altar Tears," *Journal of Religion and Abuse* (Winter 2006): 5–6. Used by permission.

Chapter 7

1. P. D. Eastman, *Are You My Mother?* (New York: Random House, 1960).

2. A fine little book that explains how to pray this way and includes five hundred Scripture texts for meditation is Thelma Hall, *Too Deep for Words: Rediscovering Lectio Divina* (New York: Paulist Press, 1988).

3. Some portions of this material on Jabez was first published as Elaine A. Heath, "Jabez, a Man Called Pain," *Ashland Theological Journal* 33 (2001): 7–16. Used by permission. Many people have become familiar with Jabez through Bruce Wilkinson, *The Prayer of Jabez* (Sisters, OR: Multnomah Press, 2000). Survivors read this story, along with the rest of the Bible, through a different lens.

4. We find a similar phenomenon in Hosea, where the prophet is commanded by Yahweh to name his children "Jezreel" (God Plants), "Lo-ruhamah" (Not Loved), and "Lo-ammi" (Not My People). Recall the naming of Jacob (Deceiver) and how he lived his name. The theme of the power of naming runs throughout the Bible.

5. A. Van Selms, "Balaam," in *New Bible Dictionary*, 2nd ed., CD-ROM (Wheaton: Tyndale, 1982; Oak Harbor, WA: Logos Research Systems, 1997).

6. J. A. Motyer, "Curse," and Van Selms, "Balaam," in *New Bible Dictionary*.

7. Fr. Van Kaam cofounded the Institute of Formative Spirituality at Duquesne University with Dr. Susan Muto. The Institute closed in 1993, but Dr. Muto continues the legacy of Fr. Van Kaam's work through the Epiphany Association. For more information about the late Fr. Van Kaam's work, see the website for the Epiphany Association and the Epiphany Lay Formation Academy at www.epiphanyassociation.org/default.asp.

8. This is only one of many passages in the Bible that contain feminine images of God. A well-known image from John 3 is the Holy Spirit as birthing Mother. Jesus tells Nicodemus that we are born of water and the Spirit.

9. Julian of Norwich, *Showings*, trans. and with an introduction by Edmund Colledge and James Walsh, Classics of Western Spirituality (New York: Paulist Press, 1978), 295.

10. In Christian theology, this is called "apophatic" spirituality, referring to the fact that God cannot be contained by any image or collection of images because God is not a created "thing." To limit God to one image is to in a certain sense idolize that image. This is why we need to know about, appreciate, and pray with all the images of God in the Bible. Each of them communicates something essential to us about God's nature. Yet all of them taken together still do not reveal the fullness of God's person. A great, divine mystery remains, requiring humility and wonder on our part.

11. *Perichoresis* is a combination of two Greeks words meaning "circle dance" and has been used since antiquity to describe the three-in-one relation-

ship of love and creativity between Father, Son, and Holy Spirit. This beautifully nuanced image is one of the Triune God engaged in an infinite, circular dance of mutually interpenetrating love, with an overflow of creative energy. Creation, salvation, sanctification, all of the work of God is perichoretic, involving the mutually self-giving, self-emptying, fierce love of the Trinity.

Chapter 8

1. Here I refer to hermaphrodite, gay, and lesbian persons.

2. F. Scott Spencer, "Eunuch," in *The New Interpreter's Dictionary of the Bible, D–H,* vol. 2 (Nashville: Abingdon, 2007), 355.

3. Ibid.

4. For more on sexual addiction, see Patrick Carnes, *Don't Call It Love: Recovery from Sexual Addiction* (New York: Bantam, 1992); Charlotte S. Kasl, *Women, Sex, and Addiction: A Search for Love and Power* (New York: Harper One, 1990); and Marnie C. Ferree, *No Stones: Women Redeemed from Sexual Shame* (Fairfax, VA: Xulon Press, 2002).

5. See Leviticus 25, for example.

6. Wendy Farley, *The Wounding and Healing of Desire: Weaving Heaven and Earth* (Louisville: Westminster John Knox, 2005), 58–59.

7. Ibid., 61.

8. Here I refer to all forms of intimacy, including friendship and healthy sexual love.

Chapter 9

1. The original purity codes are found in Leviticus, beginning with chapter 11. For Bible commentaries with detailed information about the reasons for the purity codes and their ramifications, see Nobuyoshi Kiuchi, *Leviticus,* Apollos Old Testament Commentary Series (Downers Grove, IL: IVP Academic, 2007); and Gordon J. Wenham, *Leviticus,* New International Commentary on the Old Testament (Grand Rapids: Eerdmans, 1994).

2. I am using the three narratives presented in Luke 8:26–56.

3. In verse 30, they self-identify as Legion, which was a military name for a large cohort of soldiers in the Roman army. The man was oppressed not by one but by many demonic spirits.

4. Mary Pipher, *Reviving Ophelia* (New York: Ballantine Books, 1994).

5. Ibid., 22.

Chapter 10

1. I include myself in the category of contemplatives, though I am still a beginner in many ways. The contemplative path is primarily what has brought deep healing to my wounds, in conjunction with loving friendships and appropriate counseling.

Chapter 11

1. Christology is the area of theology that focuses on the nature and mission of Christ. Soteriology focuses on the meaning of salvation. Hamartiology

deals with issues of sin and evil. Pneumatology has to do with the person and work of the Holy Spirit. Systematic theology is the school bus on which these subcategories ride to and from the theological academy and the church. There are other school buses for pastoral theology, ascetical theology, and biblical studies. Sometimes, I'm afraid, the buses don't reach their destinations and instead get stuck in the parking lot of one of the institutions.

2. See Daniel B. Schneider, "FYI," *New York Times*, May 13, 2001, http://query.nytimes.com/gst/fullpage.html?res=9A05E3DC113BF930A25756C0A9679C8B63&sec=&spon.

3. Marie M. Fortune, "Toward a Feminist Theology of Religion and the State," in *Violence against Women and Children: A Christian Theological Sourcebook*, ed. Marie M. Fortune and Carol J. Adams (New York: Continuum, 1995), 30.

4. CSI, www.cbs.com/primetime/csi.

5. Joel B. Green and Mark D. Baker, *Recovering the Scandal of the Cross: Atonement in New Testament and Contemporary Contexts* (Downers Grove, IL: InterVarsity Press, 2000). Also see the subsequent anthology of sermons by a wide array of contributors: Mark D. Baker, ed., *Proclaiming the Scandal of the Cross: Contemporary Images of Atonement* (Grand Rapids: Baker Academic, 2006).

Chapter 12

1. Marjorie Procter-Smith, *Praying with Our Eyes Open* (Nashville: Abingdon, 1995), 115, 117–24, 133–34.

2. Marjorie Procter-Smith, "The Whole Loaf: Holy Communion and Survival," in *Violence against Women and Children: A Christian Theological Sourcebook*, ed. Marie M. Fortune and Carol J. Adams (New York: Continuum, 1995).

3. For a detailed map for eucharistic reform along these lines, see June Christine Goudy, *The Feast of Our Lives: Re-imaging Communion* (Cleveland: Pilgrim Press, 2002).

4. Quoted in Morton Kelsey, *Psychology, Medicine, and Christian Healing* (New York: HarperSanFrancisco, 1988), 141. This book is a wonderful study of the history of healing in the church from the time of the New Testament through the late twentieth century. Kelsey argues for a retrieval of a strongly therapeutic theology of the Eucharist.

5. Augustine, *The City of God*, trans. Henry Bettenson (New York: Penguin, 1984), XXII.8 [Author: please check page number].

6. Just how Jesus is present in the Eucharist is a source of sharp disagreement among major Christian traditions and is beyond the focus of this book. The three primary positions are transubstantiation, consubstantiation, and memorialist, all having to do with the degree to which Christ is present in the actual bread and wine of the Eucharist. Regardless of our position on this matter, virtually all Christians who celebrate the Lord's Supper believe that Christ is uniquely present in some way as we come to the table. Thus the potential for healing in the Eucharist is available to all Christians.

7. Beguines were an unofficial monastic order for lay women, originating in the German lowlands in the thirteenth century. They were known for their emphasis on healing and work among the poor and today are noted for their "love mysticism." For more on the origins and early history of the Beguines, see Walter Simons, *Cities of Ladies: Beguine Communities in the Medieval Low Countries, 1200–1565* (Philadelphia: University of Pennsylvania Press, 2001). For more about the love mysticism and other aspects of Beguine spirituality, see Saskia Murk-Jansen, *Brides in the Desert: The Spirituality of the Beguines* (Maryknoll, NY: Orbis, 1998).

8. Hadewijch, *Hadewijch: The Complete Works*, ed. Columba Hart, Classics of Western Spirituality (New York: Paulist Press, 1980), 281.

9. These are the kinds of comments I hear when this topic comes up in spirituality classes.

10. Julia Foote, "A Brand Plucked from the Fire: An Autobiographical Sketch," in *Sisters in the Spirit: Three Black Women's Autobiographies of the Nineteenth Century*, ed. and with an introduction by William Andrews (Bloomington, IN: Indiana University Press, 1986), 202–3.

11. Janet Ruffing, *Spiritual Direction: Beyond the Beginnings* (New York: Paulist Press, 2000), 100.

12. M. Elaine McCollins Flake, *God in Her Midst: Preaching Healing for Wounded Women* (Valley Forge, PA: Judson Press, 2007); and Annie Lally Milhaven, ed., *Sermons Seldom Heard: Women Proclaim Their Lives* (New York: Crossroads, 1991).

Appendix B

1. Faith Trust Institute, "Sexual Violence and Religion," www.faithtrust institute.org/index.php?p=Sexual+Violence&s=32.

Index